Microsoft®
Excel 2013:
Level 1 of 3

ERIC A. WEINSTEIN

Suffolk County Community College

D1379119

LABYRINTH
LEARNING™

Berkeley, CA

Microsoft Excel 2013: Level 1

Copyright © 2014 by Labyrinth Learning

LABYRINTH
LEARNING™

Labyrinth Learning
2560 9th Street, Suite 320
Berkeley, California 94710
800.522.9746
On the web at lablearning.com

President:
Brian Favro

Product Development Manager:
Jason Favro

Managing Editor:
Laura Popelka

Production Editor:
Margaret Young

Production Manager:
Rad Proctor

eLearning Production Manager:
Arl S. Nadel

eLearning Development:
Judy Mardar and Andrew Vaughnley

Developmental Editors:
Trisha Conlon and Sandra Rittman

Indexing:
Joanne Sprott

Cover Design:
Mick Koller, SuperLab Design

Interior Design:
Mark Ong, Side-by-Side Studio

All rights reserved. Printed in the United States of America. No part of this material protected by this copyright notice may be reproduced or utilized in any form or by any means, electronic or mechanical, including photocopying, recording, scanning, or by information storage and retrieval systems without written permission from the copyright owner.

Labyrinth Learning™ and the Labyrinth Learning logo are trademarks of Labyrinth Learning. Microsoft® is a registered trademark of Microsoft Corporation in the United States and/or other countries and is used by Labyrinth Learning under license from owner. This title is an independent publication not affiliated with Microsoft Corporation. Other product and company names mentioned herein may be the trademarks of their respective owners.

Labyrinth Learning is independent from Microsoft Corporation, and not affiliated with Microsoft in any manner. While this publication may be used in assisting end users to prepare for a Microsoft Office Specialist exam, Microsoft, its designated program administrator, and Labyrinth Learning do not warrant that the use of this publication will ensure passing a Microsoft Office Specialist exam.

The example companies, organizations, products, people, and events depicted herein are fictitious. No association with any real company, organization, product, person, or event is intended or inferred.

Screenshots reprinted with permission.

ITEM: 1-59136-491-4
ISBN-13: 978-1-59136-491-7

Manufactured in the United States of America.

10 9 8 7 6 5 4 3 2 1

Table of Contents

Quick Reference Tables

Preface

In today's digital world, knowing how to use the most popular suite of desktop software applications is critical. Our goal is to teach new users how to take advantage of this technology and to help experienced users understand how the applications have changed from previous versions. We begin with fundamental concepts and take learners through a systematic progression of exercises, resulting in skill mastery.

An online student resource center accompanies this book. It contains Concepts Review quizzes, student exercise files, and other learning tools. The URL for the student resource center is printed on the inside front cover of this textbook.

Supplemental Options

Video Tutorials: Our easy-to-follow instructional design is complemented with hundreds of videos that demonstrate the concepts and skills covered in this textbook. All videos can be accessed online with a single license key. Videos are an option for all learners. Keys can be purchased at http://lablearning.com/Store/Shop-Videos.

eLab Course Management System: eLab is a web-based learning systems that integrates seamlessly with this textbook. eLab is an option for students enrolled in instructor-led courses that have adopted eLab as part of their course curriculum.

Visual Conventions

This book uses visual and typographic cues to guide students through the lessons. Some of these cues are described below.

Type this text	Text you type at the keyboard is printed in this typeface.
Action words	The important action words in exercise steps are presented in boldface.
Ribbon	Glossary terms are presented in black text with a blue background.
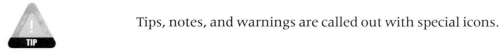	Tips, notes, and warnings are called out with special icons.
Command→ Command→ Command→ Command	Commands to execute from the Ribbon are presented like this: Ribbon Tab→Command Group→Command→Subcommand.
FROM THE KEYBOARD [Ctrl]+[S] to save	These margin notes present shortcut keys for executing certain tasks.
FROM THE RIBBON File→Save	These margin notes show Ribbon paths for executing certain tasks.

Acknowledgements

This textbook has benefited greatly from the reviews and suggestions of the following instructors.

Kim Anderson, *Elgin Community College*

Ann Blackman, *Parkland College*

Robert Caruso, *Santa Rosa Junior College*

Lori Collins, *Pike-Lincoln Technical Center*

Rose Corgan, *University of Cincinnati Blue Ash*

Julie Davis, *Mt. Diablo Adult Education (Loma Vista Adult School)*

Teresita Galvizo, *South East High*

Evangelina Garner, *South Texas Vocational Technical institute*

Reuben Gradsky, *North Carolina State University and Wake County Tech*

Michael Heath, *River Parishes Community College - Technical Education Campus*

Leonard James, *Placer School for Adults*

Ray Janosko, *Community College of Allegheny County*

Joan Johnson, *Lake Sumter Community College*

Kathy Lavieri, *Great Oaks Institute of Technology and Career Development*

Teresa Loftis, *San Bernardino Adult School*

Linda Maatta, *Davis College*

John Mims, *Central New Mexico Community College Workforce Training Center*

Kay Nelson, *The Lifelong Learning Center, Missoula County Public Schools*

Monika Olsen, *Acalanes Adult Education*

Diane Perreault, *Sacramento City College*

Kari Phillips, *Davis Applied Technology College*

Sonya Sample, *Greenville Technical College*

Maryla Scarpa, *Vincennes University Jasper*

Jeff Stern, *Sheridan Technical Center*

Mary Jo Slater, *Community College of Beaver County*

Cynthia Wade, *CierraTEC*

Ali Ware, *Humboldt County Office of Education*

Microsoft® Excel 2013:
Level 1 of 3

Exploring Excel 2013

LEARNING OBJECTIVES

After studying this lesson, you will be able to:

- Explain how Excel can help your productivity
- Navigate the Excel window and issue commands
- Enter text and numbers in cells
- Distinguish between a text and a number entry in a cell
- Save, "save as," and close workbooks

In this lesson, you will develop fundamental Excel skills. This lesson will provide you with a solid understanding of Excel so you are prepared to master advanced features later. You will learn how to navigate around a worksheet, enter various types of data, select cells, and save your work.

Building a Basic Worksheet

Welcome to Green Clean, a janitorial product supplier and cleaning service contractor to small businesses, shopping plazas, and office buildings. Green Clean uses environmentally friendly cleaning products and incorporates sustainability practices wherever possible, including efficient energy and water use, recycling and waste reduction, and reduced petroleum use in vehicles. In addition to providing green cleaning services, the company also sells its eco-friendly products directly to customers.

You need to create a list of hours that cleaning service employees worked during the weekend (Friday through Sunday). Your manager has asked you to compile the data from employee time sheets and report hours on a daily basis. Your worksheet is shown in the following illustration.

	A	B	C	D	E
1	Service Employees Weekend Hours Worked				
2					
3	Alton Mall		Friday	Saturday	Sunday
4		Barnes	6	6	6
5		Chau	8	8	8
6		Lee	4	0	4
7		Olsen	4	3	0
8		Total Hrs			
9	Century Bank				
10		Garcia	3	5	0
11		Kimura	3	4	0
12		Tan	3	5	0
13		Total Hrs			
14	Newport Medical				
15		Kowalski	8	6	8
16		Silva	6	6	0
17		Wilson	5	2	5
18		Total Hrs			

Excel makes it easy for you to organize your data in columns and rows.

Presenting Excel 2013

Video Library   http://labyrinthelab.com/videos   Video Number: EX13-V0101

Microsoft Office Excel is an electronic worksheet program that allows you to work with numbers and data much more efficiently than the pen-and-paper method. Excel is used in virtually all industries and many households for a variety of tasks such as:

- Creating and maintaining detailed budgets
- Performing "what-if" scenarios and break-even analyses
- Producing detailed charts to graphically display information
- Creating invoices or purchase orders
- Working with reports exported from small business accounting software programs such as Intuit's QuickBooks®

As you can see, Excel is a powerful program that is used not only to work with numbers but also to maintain databases. In fact, if you have started a database in Excel, you can even import it into Microsoft Access (the Microsoft Office Suite database program). Many people use Excel to track their databases rather than Access because of its ease of use and because Access is not included in all of the Microsoft Office editions.

Starting Excel

The method you use to start Excel and other Office 2013 applications depends on whether you are using the Windows 7 or Windows 8 operating system.

Windows 7
- Click the Start 🪟 button, choose Microsoft Office 2013 from the All Programs menu, and then choose Excel 2013 or another Office 2013 application.

Windows 8
- Locate the tile labeled Excel 2013 on the Windows Start screen, and then click the tile to start Excel.

Start Excel

In this exercise, you will start your computer and open Microsoft Excel. If you are using Windows 7, follow the steps below the Windows 7 heading. If you are using Windows 8, follow the steps below the Windows 8 heading.

1. If necessary, start your computer.

   The Windows Desktop (Windows 7) or Start screen (Windows 8) appears. Now, follow the steps for your version of Windows.

Windows 7

2. Click the Start button at the left edge of the taskbar and choose **All Programs**.

3. Choose **Microsoft Office 2013**, and then choose **Excel 2013** from the menu.

4. Make sure the Excel window is **maximized** .

5. Click the **Blank Workbook** template to open the Excel window.

Windows 8

6. Locate, and then click the **Excel 2013 tile**.

7. Make sure the Excel window is **maximized** .

   The program loads and the Excel Start screen appears.

8. Click the **Blank Workbook** template to open the Excel window.

Exploring the Excel Program Window

Video Library   http://labyrinthelab.com/videos   Video Number: EX13-V0102

When you start Excel, you will see a blank workbook displayed. The following illustration describes important objects in the Excel program window.

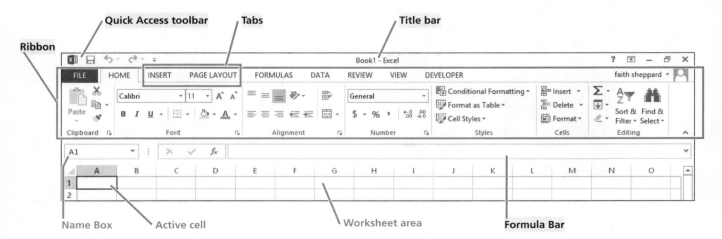

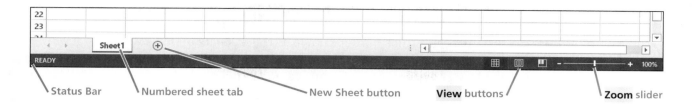

Status Bar   Numbered sheet tab   New Sheet button   **View** buttons   **Zoom** slider

Using Worksheets and Workbooks

Video Library   http://labyrinthelab.com/videos   Video Number: EX13-V0103

A workbook is a file containing one or more worksheets. Excel displays a blank workbook with a single worksheet when you start the program. Worksheets are represented by tabs at the bottom of the screen. One tab will be shown for each worksheet within the workbook. New sheets can be added by clicking the New Sheet button. You can enter text, numbers, formulas, charts, and other objects within these worksheets.

FROM THE RIBBON
File→New→ Blank Workbook

FROM THE KEYBOARD
Ctrl+N to open a new workbook

Excel 2013

| **Annual** | Winter | Spring | Summer | Fall | ⊕ |

Here, worksheet tabs organize annual and seasonal data.

The terms *spreadsheet* and *worksheet* can be used interchangeably.

A worksheet has a grid structure with 1,048,576 horizontal rows and 16,384 vertical columns, though only a small number of rows and columns are visible at one time. The intersection of each row and column is referred to as a cell. A cell reference is composed of a column letter and row number. For example, A1 is the reference for the cell in the top-left corner of the worksheet, at the intersection of column A and row 1.

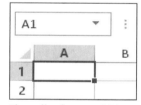

The cell reference A1 is displayed in the Name Box.

Mousing Around in Excel

The shape of the mouse pointer will change as you move it around the Excel window. The pointer shape determines what happens when you click or drag on a cell or object.

Mouse Pointer Shape	Function
⊹	Click to select a cell; drag to select multiple cells.
✛	Drag the fill handle (bottom-right corner of a cell) to fill adjacent cells with a series of numbers, dates, etc.
↖	Click to perform many tasks including issuing a command from the Ribbon or selecting a new tab.
✛⃨	Drag selected cell contents to another location.
↕ ↔ ⤡	Drag the resize pointers to change the height and/or width of objects such as pictures, shapes, or charts.
⇥ ⬇	Select a row or column.
I	Click the I-beam pointer to enter text in locations such as the Formula Bar.

The Active Cell and the Highlight

When you click in a cell a thick border known as the *highlight* appears within that cell. The cell containing the highlight is known as the *active cell* and we often refer to that cell as being selected. The active cell is important because data or objects you enter are inserted in or near the active cell.

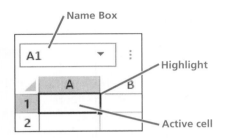

Scrolling Along in a Worksheet

The Excel window contains both vertical and horizontal scroll bars. They allow you to view other areas of the worksheet without changing the active cell. There are three ways to use the scroll bars to view other areas of your worksheet.

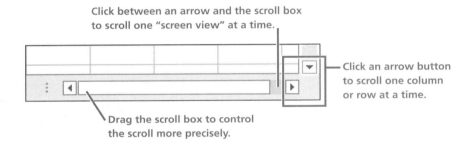

Navigating in a Worksheet

You can change the active cell by clicking in another cell, using the keyboard, or entering a cell reference in the Name Box. The vertical and horizontal scroll bars let you scroll through a worksheet; however, scrolling does not change the active cell. After scrolling, you need to change the active cell before you can enter data into that cell. The following table lists keystrokes that can be used to change the active cell.

You may type a cell reference in the Name Box and then tap Enter to navigate to that cell.

Keystroke(s)	How the Active Cell Changes
→ ← ↑ ↓	One cell right, left, up, or down
Home	Beginning (column A) of current row
Ctrl + Home	Home cell, usually cell A1
Ctrl + End	Last cell in active part of worksheet
Page Down	Down one visible screen
Page Up	Up one visible screen
Alt + Page Down	One visible screen right
Alt + Page Up	One visible screen left
Ctrl + G	Displays Go To dialog box; enter cell reference and click OK

Excel 2013

Customizing the Ribbon

The Customize Ribbon category in Excel Options allows you to rearrange the tab order, create a new tab, add a new group to an existing tab, add or remove commands, and export all customizations for use on other computers. The built-in tabs cannot be removed, but they may be hidden. An individual tab or all tabs and the Quick Access toolbar may be reset to their original default items.

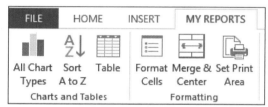

A custom tab named My Reports added to the Ribbon with commands grouped according to the user's preference and workflow.

DEVELOP YOUR SKILLS EX01-D02

Navigate and Explore the Excel Window

In this exercise, you will navigate in a worksheet by scrolling, using the keyboard, and using the Name Box.

1. Slide the mouse pointer and notice the thick **cross shape** ✚ when it is in the worksheet area.

   If you click with this pointer shape, you will change the active cell.

2. Click any cell and notice that the highlight appears around that cell.

   This is now the active cell.

3. Change the active cell five times by clicking in various cells.

   Now you will learn how to use the keyboard to move around a worksheet.

4. Use the →, ←, ↑, and ↓ keys to position the highlight in **cell F10**.

5. Tap Home and see that the highlight moves to **cell A10**.

    The Home key always makes active the cell in column A of the current row.

6. Press Ctrl + Home to move the highlight to **cell A1**.

7. Tap Page Down three times.

    Notice that Excel displays the next 25 or so rows (one "visible" screen's worth) each time you tap Page Down.

8. Press and hold ↑ until **cell A1** is the active cell.

Use the Scroll Bars

The scroll bars allow you to see other portions of the Excel worksheet area without changing the active cell.

9. Click the **Scroll Right** ▶ button on the horizontal scroll bar until columns AA and AB are visible.

    Excel labels the first 26 columns A–Z and the next 26 columns AA–AZ. A similar labeling scheme is used for the remaining columns out to the final column, XFD.

10. Click the **Scroll Down** ▼ button on the vertical scroll bar until row 100 is visible.

    Notice that cell A1 remains displayed in the Name Box, as the highlight has not moved. To move the highlight, you must click in a cell or use the keyboard.

Use the Go To Command

11. Press Ctrl + G to display the Go To dialog box, type **g250** in the Reference box, and click **OK**.

    Keep in mind that cell references are not case sensitive so you can enter the letters in either upper or lower case.

12. Use the **Go To** command to move to three different cells.

13. Press Ctrl + Home to return to **cell A1**.

14. Follow these steps to navigate with the Name Box:

    Ⓐ Click in the **Name Box** at the left end of the Formula Bar.

    Ⓑ Type **ab9** and tap Enter.

    The highlight should now be in cell AB9.

15. Press Ctrl + Home to return to **cell A1**.

16. Follow these steps to explore the Excel window:

Ⓐ Click the **New Sheet** button.

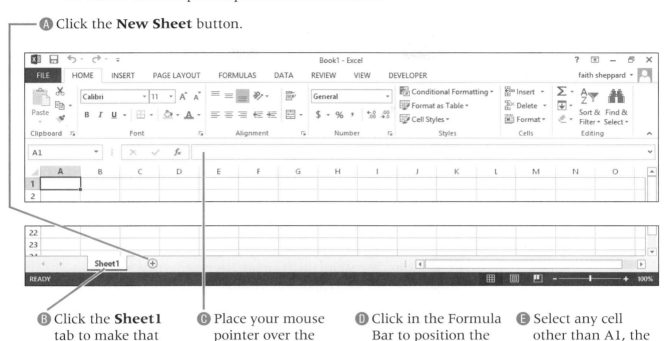

Ⓑ Click the **Sheet1** tab to make that sheet active.

Ⓒ Place your mouse pointer over the **Formula Bar** and notice it changes to an I-beam shape.

Ⓓ Click in the Formula Bar to position the flashing insertion point in the Formula Bar.

Ⓔ Select any cell other than A1, the currently active cell, to exit the Formula Bar.

17. Select **cell A1**.

Leave the Excel window open.

Entering Data in Excel

Video Library   http://labyrinthelab.com/videos   Video Number: EX13-V0104

Within Excel, data is entered into the active cell. Text is used for descriptive headings, and entries that require alphabetic characters. Numbers can be entered directly or can be calculated using formulas. Excel recognizes the data you enter and decides whether the entry is text, a number, or a formula that performs a calculation.

Data Types

Entries are defined as one of two main classifications: constant values or formulas. Constant values can be text, numeric, or a combination of both, and they do not change when other worksheet information changes. Conversely, formula entries display the results of calculations, and a result can change when a value in another cell changes.

| f_x | 1263 | A constant value | f_x | =SUM(C5:C8) | A formula |

Completing Cell Entries

Text and numbers are entered by positioning the highlight in the desired cell, typing the desired text or number, and completing the entry. You can use ⌈Enter⌉, ⌈Tab⌉, or any of the arrow keys (⌈→⌉, ⌈←⌉, ⌈↑⌉, ⌈↓⌉) to complete an entry. The method you use to complete the entry will determine where the active cell moves.

Entry Completion Method	Where the Active Cell Will Appear
⌈Enter⌉	It will move down to the next cell.
⌈Tab⌉	It will move to the next cell to the right.
⌈→⌉ ⌈↑⌉ ⌈↓⌉ ⌈←⌉	It will move to the next cell in the direction of the arrow key.
⌈Esc⌉	The entry will be deleted and the current cell will remain active.

The Enter and Cancel Buttons

The Enter and Cancel buttons appear on the Formula Bar whenever you enter or edit an entry. The Enter button completes the entry and keeps the highlight in the current cell. The Cancel button cancels the entry, as does the ⌈Esc⌉ key.

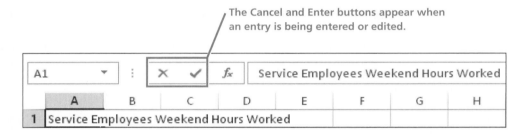

The Cancel and Enter buttons appear when an entry is being entered or edited.

Deleting and Replacing Entries

You can delete an entire entry after it has been completed by clicking in the cell and tapping ⌈Delete⌉. Likewise, you can replace an entry by clicking in the cell and typing a new entry.

Long Text Entries

Text entries often do not fit in a cell. These entries are known as long entries. Excel will either display the long entry over the adjacent cell (if the cell to the right of the long entry is empty), or Excel will shorten, or truncate, the display of the long entry (if the cell to the right of the long entry is in use.) In this latter instance, the entire long entry remains within the cell, but it is not fully visible. You can widen a column to accommodate a long entry.

	A	B	C	D	E
1	Service Employees Weekend Hours Worked				
2					

This is a long entry. The entire phrase is entered in cell A1, although it displays over the range A1:E1.

Enter Text

In this exercise, you will enter text, including long entries, and will use various keystrokes to complete entries.

1. Make **cell A1** active by clicking the **mouse pointer** ⊹ in it.

2. Type **Service Employees Weekend Hours Worked**, and then tap ⌷Enter⌷.

   The text is entered in the cell and the highlight moves down to cell A2. Notice that the entry displays over cells B1, C1, D1, and E1, although the entire entry still belongs to cell A1.

3. Click **cell A1** and note the appearance of the Formula Bar.

   Notice that the Formula Bar displays the name of the active cell (A1) as well as its content.

4. Tap ⌷→⌷ to make cell B1 active.

5. Look at the **Formula Bar** and notice that cell B1 is empty.

   The long entry belongs to cell A1 even though it is displayed over the range A1:E1.

Type Additional Text Entries

6. Click in **cell C3**.

7. Type **Friday** and tap ⌷→⌷ once.

   Notice that the entry is completed and the highlight moves to cell D3.

8. Type **Wednesday** in **cell D3** and tap ⌷→⌷.

9. Type **Sunday** in **cell E3** and tap ⌷←⌷.

   Notice that the display of Wednesday *is shortened, or truncated.*

Friday	Wednesd	Sunday

10. Type **Saturday** in **cell D3** and tap ⌷Enter⌷.

    The new entry in cell D3 replaces the previous entry.

Excel 2013

11. Enter the remaining text entries shown here.

If Excel proposes any entries for you as you type, simply continue typing.

	A	B	C	D	E
1	Service Employees Weekend Hours Worked				
2					
3	Alton Mall		Friday	Saturday	Sunday
4		Barnes			
5		Chau			
6		Lee			
7		Olsen			
8		Total Hrs			
9	Century Bank				
10		Garcia			
11		Kimura			
12		Tan			
13		Total Hrs			
14	Newport Medical				
15		Kowalski			
16		Silva			
17		Wilson			
18		Total Hrs			

Working with Numbers

Video Library   http://labyrinthelab.com/videos   Video Number: EX13-V0105

Number entries can contain only the digits 0–9 and a few other characters. Excel initially right-aligns numbers in cells, although you can change this alignment. The following table lists characters that Excel accepts as part of a number entry.

Valid Characters in Number Entries
The digits 0-9
The following characters: + - ( ) , / $ % . *

Entering numbers using the numeric keypad is more efficient than using the number keys at the top of the keyboard.

Number Formats

It isn't necessary to type commas, dollar signs, and other number formats when entering numbers. Instead, you can use Excel's formatting commands to add the desired number formats.

Decimals and Negative Numbers

You should always type a decimal point if the number you are entering requires one. Likewise, you should precede a negative number entry with a minus (–) sign or enclose it in parentheses ( ).

Enter Numbers

In this exercise, you will practice entering numbers and canceling entries before completion.

1. Position the highlight in **cell C4** and type **6**, but don't complete the entry.

2. Look at the Formula Bar and notice the **Cancel** ☒ and **Enter** ☑ buttons.
   These buttons appear whenever you begin entering or editing data in a cell.

3. Click **Enter** ☑ to complete the entry.
   Notice that the highlight remains in cell C4.

Use the Cancel Button and the ⌨Esc Key

	A	B	C	D	E
1	Service Employees Weekend Hours Worked				
2					
3	Alton Mall		Friday	Saturday	Sunday
4		Barnes	6	6	6
5		Chau	8	8	8
6		Lee	4	0	4
7		Olsen	4	3	0
8		Total Hrs			
9	Century Bank				
10		Garcia	3	5	0
11		Kimura	3	4	0
12		Tan	3	5	0
13		Total Hrs			
14	Newport Medical				
15		Kowalski	8	6	8
16		Silva	6	6	0
17		Wilson	5	2	5
18		Total Hrs			

4. Position the highlight in **cell C5** and type **8**, but don't complete the entry.

5. Click **Cancel** ☒ on the Formula Bar.

6. Type **8** again, and this time tap ⌨Esc.
   The ⌨Esc key has the same effect as the Cancel button.

Excel 2013

7. Type **8** once again, and this time tap ⬇.

   Notice that Excel right-aligns the number in the cell.

8. Enter the remaining numbers shown on the prior page.

To use the numeric keypad to enter numbers, the Number Lock light, which is included on most keyboards, must be on. If it's not, press the ⎡Num Lock⎤ key on the keypad.

Understanding Save Concepts

Video Library   http://labyrinthelab.com/videos   Video Number: EX13-V0106

One important lesson to learn is to save your workbooks every 10–15 minutes, in order to avoid losing data as a result of power outages and careless accidents. Workbooks are saved to file storage locations such as a USB drive, the Documents folder, a shared network drive, and websites on the Internet. When a worksheet is first saved, the Save As dialog box appears so that you can assign a name, and location on the computer, to your file. If the worksheet has already been saved and you choose the Save command, Excel replaces the previous version with the new edited version.

FROM THE RIBBON
File→Save

FROM THE KEYBOARD
⎡Ctrl⎤+⎡S⎤ to save

FROM THE RIBBON
File→Save As

FROM THE KEYBOARD
⎡Alt⎤, ⎡F⎤, ⎡A⎤ or ⎡F12⎤ to save as

Issuing Commands from the Keyboard

While commands are always available on the ribbon, it can be more efficient to issue them from the keyboard. Try to use both the keyboard shortcuts that are highlighted throughout this text and the key tips that display when the ⎡Alt⎤ key is tapped.

QUICK REFERENCE	SAVING A WORKBOOK AND MANAGING WORKBOOK FILE VERSIONS
Task	**Procedure**
Save for the first time	■ Click Save 💾 on the Quick Access toolbar, choose Computer, and choose Browse. ■ Name the workbook, choose the save location, and click Save.
Save changes in the workbook	■ Click Save 💾 on the Quick Access toolbar.
Save in a new location or with a new name	■ Choose File→Save As, choose Computer, and choose Browse. ■ Change the name of the workbook, the file storage location, or both, and click Save.
Save the workbook in the Excel 97-2003 Format	■ Choose File→Save As, choose Computer, choose Browse, enter the filename, and navigate to the desired file storage location. ■ Choose Excel 97-2003 from the Save as Type list, and click Save.
Use key tips to choose a command	■ Tap the ⎡Alt⎤ key to display key tips. ■ Tap the letter or number key that corresponds to the desired tab on the Ribbon or Quick Access toolbar button, and tap the letter(s) in the key tip for the desired command on the Ribbon.

DEVELOP YOUR SKILLS EX01-D05

Save the Workbook

In this exercise, you will save the workbook you have been working on. You will also use key tips to select a command on the Ribbon and view Excel's options for saving workbooks.

***Before You Begin:** Navigate to the student resource center to download the student exercise files for this book.*

1. Click the **Save** button on the Quick Access toolbar, choose **Computer**, and choose **Browse**.

   The Save As dialog box appears because this is the first time you are saving the workbook.

2. Navigate to your file storage location.

   Notice that the proposed name Book1 (something similar, such as Book 2, may be displayed on your screen) appears in the File Name Box.

3. Type **`EX01-D05-WeekendHours-[FirstInitialLastName]`** to replace the proposed name.

   Replace the bracketed text with your first initial and last name. For example, if your name is Bethany Smith, your filename would look like this: EX01-D05-WeekendHours-BSmith.

4. Click **Save** or tap Enter.

   Notice that the filename appears in the Title Bar of the window to indicate that the workbook is saved.

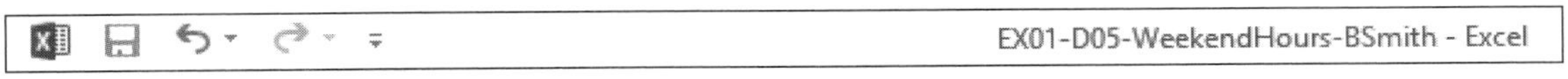

Use Key Tips to Save As

5. Tap Alt.

   Key tips display on the Quick Access toolbar and Ribbon.

6. Tap F.

   The File tab displays with the Info tab selected.

7. Tap A.

   The Save As tab displays.

8. Tap B.

   The Save As dialog box displays.

9. Tap Esc to cancel the dialog box without saving.

10. Tap ESC again to return to the active worksheet.

    Leave the workbook open for the next exercise.

Closing Workbooks

Video Library   http://labyrinthelab.com/videos   Video Number: EX13-V0107

The Close command is used to close an open workbook. When you close a workbook that has not been saved, Excel prompts you to save the changes. If you choose to save at the prompt and the workbook has previously been saved, Excel simply saves the changes and closes the workbook. If the workbook is new, Excel displays the Save As dialog box, allowing you to assign a name and file storage location to the workbook. Any other workbooks that are being used will remain open until you close them or exit Excel.

DEVELOP YOUR SKILLS EX01-D06
Close the Workbook and Start a New Workbook

In this exercise, you will close the workbook that you have been working on throughout this lesson.

1. Choose **File→Close**.

2. Click the **Save** or **Yes** button if Excel asks you if you want to save the changes.

   Notice that no workbook appears in the Excel window. The Excel window always has this appearance when all workbooks have been closed.

3. Click **Close** ⊠. Exit **Excel**.

   The Excel window has now closed as well.

Concepts Review

To check your knowledge of the key concepts introduced in this lesson, complete the Concepts Review quiz by choosing the appropriate access option below.

If you are...	Then access the quiz by...
Using the Labyrinth Video Library	Going to http://labyrinthelab.com/videos
Using eLab	Logging in, choosing Content, and navigating to the Concepts Review quiz for this lesson
Not using the Labyrinth Video Library or eLab	Going to the student resource center for this book

Reinforce Your Skills

Use Excel 2013

In this exercise, you will start Excel and examine various elements of the program.

Present and Start Excel

1. Consider the different tasks that you perform when completing classwork. Think about ways your work could be minimized through the use of Excel.

   As you complete the remaining steps for this exercise, keep in mind these potential benefits.

2. Follow your step for the version of Windows you are running:

   ■ **Windows 7:** Choose **Start→All Programs→Microsoft Office 2013→Excel 2013→Blank Workbook**.

   ■ **Windows 8:** Choose **Excel 2013 tile→Blank Workbook**.

   Notice that in either case a blank workbook is displayed when you open Excel.

Explore the Excel Window

3. Ensure that **cell A1** is selected.

   Notice that the name bar displays the name of the active cell.

4. Click **Scroll Down** ▾ to scroll down to row 100

5. Click **cell B100**.

   The Name Box now displays the name of the new active cell.

6. Press ⌃Ctrl⌄ + ⌃Home⌄ to return to cell A1.

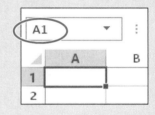

Work with Tabs and Ribbons

7. Click the **Data** tab on the Ribbon.

   Look at the types of commands available. Many of them will be covered in later lessons of this book.

8. Click the **View** tab.

9. Click the **Collapse the Ribbon** ⌃ button at the upper-right corner of the window.

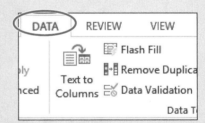

10. Click the **Home** tab to display the Ribbon once again.

The Home tab is displayed because you chose it to redisplay the Ribbon.

11. Click the **Pin the Ribbon** button to permanently display the Ribbon once again.

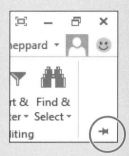

12. Click the **Customize Quick Access Toolbar** button.

13. Add the **Quick Print** button to the toolbar by selecting it from the menu that appears.

14. Use the `Print Screen` key on your keyboard, and paste the screen into a Microsoft Word document.

The Print Screen key makes a copy of the entire screen (although no indication of this can be seen within Excel), which can then be pasted in a variety of programs.

15. Save the Word document as **EX01-R01-ScreenShot-[FirstInitialLastName]** in the **EX2013 Lesson 01** folder. Exit **Word** and **Excel**.

16. Submit your final file based on the guidelines provided by your instructor.

To view examples of how your file or files should look at the end of this exercise, go to the student resource center.

REINFORCE YOUR SKILLS EX01-R02
Enter and Save Data

In this exercise, you will create and save a simple spreadsheet.

Enter Data

1. Start **Excel**. Open a blank workbook.

2. Enter text in **rows 1 through 10** as shown.

Use `Tab` and `Enter` as necessary to enter the data. Type the customer's name and address in cells B6, B7, and B8.

	A	B	C	D	E
1	Kids for Change				
2	Order Tracking Worksheet				
3					
4	Order No.	1552			
5					
6	Sold to:	Empire Dry Cleaning			
7		1833 Franklin Highway			
8		Huntington, WV 25716			
9					
10	Item	In Stock?	Quantity	Price	Discount

Work with Numbers

3. In **cells A11–E15,** enter the data shown here.

   Type a decimal point (.) in the Price and Discount columns, where displayed. Type a minus (–) sign before the numbers in the Discount column.

◢	A	B	C	D	E
10	Item	In Stock?	Quantity	Price	Discount
11	A423	Y	2	63.95	-3.15
12	A321	Y	4	28.95	0
13	D928	N	16	5.85	-0.59
14	S251	N	8	3.09	-0.31
15	B444	Y	20	8.77	-0.88

Employ Save Concepts

4. Choose **Save** 🖫 on the Quick Access toolbar, and then choose **Computer→Browse**.

5. Type `EX01-R02-OrderTracking-[FirstInitialLastName]` and navigate to your **EX2013 Lesson 01** folder.

6. Click **Save** or tap ⎡Enter⎤.

   The workbook is saved in the location that you specified.

Close and Start a New Workbook

7. Select **File→Close**.

8. Select **File→New→Blank workbook**.

Exit from Excel

9. Click **Close** ⎡×⎤ to close Excel.

   As you haven't yet entered data into this workbook, Excel closes without asking you to save.

10. Submit your final file based on the guidelines provided by your instructor.

    To view examples of how your file or files should look at the end of this exercise, go to the student resource center.

REINFORCE YOUR SKILLS EX01-R03

Explore Excel 2013

In this exercise, you will enter data into a new workbook.

Present and Start Excel

1. Think back to spreadsheets you have used in the past that likely originated from Excel.

   As you focus on this in the future, you will be surprised to see how many uses there are for Excel.

2. Follow your step for the version of Windows you are running:

   ■ **Windows 7:** Choose **Start→All Programs→Microsoft Office 2013→Excel 2013→Blank workbook**.

   ■ **Windows 8:** Choose **Excel 2013 tile→Blank workbook**.

   In both instances you are presented with a blank Excel worksheet.

Explore the Excel Window

3. Select **cell B3**.

    The Name Box displays the name of the active cell.

4. Use the **Scroll Right** ▶ button to scroll to **column Z**.

    Notice that the next column is named "AA." You will get accustomed to the order of the column names as you use them more frequently.

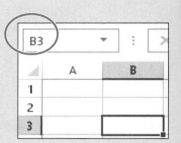

5. Click **cell Z1**.

    The name bar now displays the name of the new active cell.

6. Click Home to return to **cell A1**.

    Remember that Home brings you to column A within your current row.

Work with Tabs and Ribbons

7. Click the **Page Layout** tab on the Ribbon.

    Look at the types of commands available. Many of them will be covered in later lessons of this book.

8. Click the **Review** tab.

9. Click the **Customize Quick Access Toolbar** button.

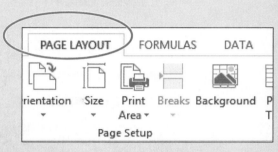

10. Add the **New** button to the toolbar by selecting it from the menu that appears.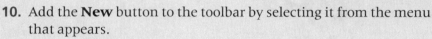

11. Click **Collapse the Ribbon** ⌃ at the upper-right corner of the window.

12. Click the **Insert** tab to display the Ribbon once again.

Notice that the Insert tab is displayed because you chose it to redisplay the Ribbon.

13. Click **Pin the Ribbon** to permanently display the Ribbon once again.

Enter Data

14. Enter text in **rows 1–8** as shown.

	A	B	C	D
1	Kids for Change			
2	Expense Listing			
3				
4		January	February	March
5	Rent			
6	Utilities			
7	Supplies			
8	Cable			

Use Tab *and* Enter *as necessary to enter the data. Type the months in cells B4, C4, and D4.*

Work with Numbers

15. In the **range B5:D8**, enter the data shown.

4		January	February	March
5	Rent	$350	$350	$350
6	Utilities	$120	$110	$145
7	Supplies	$60	$95	$75
8	Cable	$100	$100	$100

Employ Save Concepts

16. Click **Save** 🖫 on the Quick Access toolbar, and then choose **Computer→Browse**.

17. Type **EX01-R03-ExpenseTracking-[FirstInitialLastName]** then navigate to your **EX2013 Lesson 01** folder.

18. Click **Save** or tap Enter.

The workbook is saved in the location that you specified.

Close and Start a New Workbook

19. Select **File→Close**.

20. Select **File→New→Blank workbook**.

Exit from Excel

21. Click **Close** ⌧ to close Excel.

22. Submit your final file based on the guidelines provided by your instructor.

Apply Your Skills

Examine Excel Features

In this exercise, you will navigate through a variety of features within a blank Excel workbook.

Open and Explore a Blank Worksheet

1. Start **Excel** and open a **Blank Workbook**.

2. Select **cell V87** by scrolling through the worksheet.

Utilize and Alter the Ribbon

3. Select the **Formulas** tab on the Ribbon.

4. Collapse the Ribbon.

5. Add the **Spelling** button to the Quick Access toolbar.

6. Use the **Print Screen** key on your keyboard, and then paste the screen into a Microsoft Word document.

7. Save the Word document as **EX01-A01-RibbonWork-[FirstInitialLastName]** in your **EX2013 Lesson 01** folder.

8. Submit your file based on the guidelines provided by your instructor.

   To view examples of how your file or files should look at the end of this exercise, go to the student resource center.

Create a New Workbook

In this exercise, you will create a new worksheet, enter data, and then save and close the worksheet.

Enter Data and Numbers

1. Open a **Blank Worksheet**.

2. Create the worksheet shown here.

	A	B	C	D	E
1	Universal Corporate Events			Q1 Expenses	
2					
3	Item		January	February	March
4	Building	Lease	3000	3000	3000
5		Utilities	1689	1572	1646
6		Phone	250	242	329
7		Insurance	8696	0	0
8		Total			
9					
10	Equipment		1211	506	4890
11					
12	Salaries	Mgmt	4500	4500	4500
13		Full Time	20658	19777	21422
14		Part Time	24656	25980	25316
15		Total			
16					
17	Supplies	Office	1963	2432	1784
18		Vehicle	872	944	903
19		Total			
20					
21	Other	Fuel			
22		Adver.	500	300	200
23		Uniforms	63	101	83
24		Misc	162	471	65
25		Total			

Proofread all data. You will not create formulas to calculate totals in this exercise.

Close the Workbook and Exit Excel

3. Save the workbook as **EX01-A02-Q1Expenses-[FirstInitialLastName]** in your **EX2013 Lesson 01** folder.

4. Close **Excel**.

5. Submit your final file based on the guidelines provided by your instructor.

   To view examples of how your file or files should look at the end of this exercise, go to the student resource center.

Adjust the Ribbon and Build a Worksheet

In this exercise, you will create and save a new workbook.

Open and Explore a Blank Worksheet

1. Open a **Blank Worksheet**.

2. Use a single keystroke to scroll down one visible screen.

Utilize and Alter the Ribbon

3. Click the **Data** tab on the Ribbon.

4. Add the **Print Preview and Print** button to the Quick Access toolbar.

5. Collapse the Ribbon.

Enter Data and Numbers

6. Create the worksheet shown in the following illustration.

	A	B	C	D	E
1	Universal Corporate Events			Q2 Revenues	
2					
3	Type		April	May	June
4	Consult	Dept. A	5500	7500	6000
5		Dept. B	3000	2500	2500
6		Dept. C	9000	12000	4500
7		Dept. D	1500	300	3200
8		Total			
9					
10	Sales	Branch A	7000	8000	8000
11		Branch B	4200	3700	4000
12		Total			

7. Save the workbook as **EX01-A03-Q2Revenues-[FirstInitialLastName]** in your **EX2013 Lesson 01** folder.

8. Close **Excel**.

9. Submit your final file based on the guidelines provided by your instructor.

Extend Your Skills

In the course of working through the Extend Your Skills exercises, you will think critically as you use the skills taught in the lesson to complete the assigned projects. To evaluate your mastery and completion of the exercises, your instructor may use a rubric, with which more points are allotted according to performance characteristics. (The more you do, the more you earn!) Ask your instructor how your work will be evaluated.

EX01-E01 That's the Way I See It

You are known as the neighborhood Excel expert for small businesses! By request, you have created the first draft of a worksheet containing employee timesheet hours for the community's most popular bakery. The worksheet contains all necessary data, as the employees have already entered their hours. Before presenting the worksheet to the bakery, you want to review it with an eye toward layout and, of course, you want to check the spelling throughout.

Start Excel, and then open **EX01-E01-Bakery** from the **EX2013 Lesson 01** folder and save it as **EX01-E01-Bakery-[FirstInitialLastName]**.

Enter the name of your local bakery at the top, and then review the data included. Using your own literacy skills, manually make changes to the worksheet in order to correct spelling errors.

You will be evaluated based on the inclusion of all elements specified, your ability to follow directions, your ability to apply newly learned skills to a real-world situation, your creativity, and the relevance of your topic and/or data choice(s). Submit your final file based on the guidelines provided by your instructor.

EX01-E02 Be Your Own Boss

In this exercise, you will create a telephone listing for your new company, Blue Jean Landscaping. This unique business saves its customers money by allowing them to "get their hands dirty" with the physical landscaping work. As you are starting your business, this listing will allow all employees to stay in contact with one another.

Open a blank worksheet and save it as **EX01-E02-Telephone-[FirstInitialLastName]** in the **EX2013 Lesson 01** folder.

(206) 555-7164,	Stephen Samuels
(425) 555-9138,	Billy Mitchell
(206) 555-6180,	Warren Kennedy
(206) 555-1148,	Abraham Sorenson
(253) 555-0346,	Peter Smith
(425) 555-2315,	Stanley Bogart

To the right is the contact information that you will need to create the telephone listing. Make sure to structure the telephone listing in a logical manner, consistent with the skills you have learned in this lesson. At a minimum it should contain appropriate headers for each column.

Expand your telephone listing to include each employee's birthday and nickname (make them up) to make the file a more robust and useful reference.

You will be evaluated based on the inclusion of all elements specified, your ability to follow directions, your ability to apply newly learned skills to a real-world situation, your creativity, and your demonstration of an entrepreneurial spirit. Submit your final file based on the guidelines provided by your instructor.

Transfer Your Skills

In the course of working through the Transfer Your Skills exercises, you will use critical-thinking and creativity skills to complete the assigned projects using skills taught in the lesson. To evaluate your mastery and completion of the exercises, your instructor may use a rubric, with which more points are allotted according to performance characteristics. (The more you do, the more you earn!) Ask your instructor how your work will be evaluated.

EX01-T01 Use the Web as a Learning Tool

Throughout this book, you will be provided with an opportunity to use the Internet as a learning tool by completing WebQuests. According to the original creators of WebQuests, as described on their website (WebQuest.org), a WebQuest is "an inquiry-oriented activity in which most or all of the information used by learners is drawn from the web." To complete the WebQuest projects in this book, navigate to the student resource center and choose the WebQuest for the lesson on which you are currently working. The subject of each WebQuest will be relevant to the material found in the lesson.

WebQuest Subject: Design elements of a high-quality Excel worksheet

Submit your final file based on the guidelines provided by your instructor.

EX01-T02 Demonstrate Proficiency

During its first month of operations, Stormy BBQ has begun working with a number of corporate clients. These clients place multiple catering orders each month. The contact person for each client, and the revenue received from each, are as follows: Max Kenton, $5,000; Katy Super, $7,000; Chandra Shuff, $2,000; Sofia Burgoyne, $14,000; and Kenya Polasek, $6,500. In order to track the monthly revenue you will create a worksheet containing these figures, listing the clients from greatest to least revenue generated.

Open a blank worksheet and save it as **EX01-T02-StormyRevenue-[FirstInitialLastName]** in the **EX2013 Lesson 01** folder. Use the worksheet techniques learned in this lesson to track the monthly revenue, listing the clients from greatest to least revenue generated. Make sure that the worksheet is well-structured and easily readable.

Submit your final file based on the guidelines provided by your instructor.

EXCEL 2013
Editing Worksheets

LESSON OUTLINE

Opening Workbooks
Editing Entries
Selecting Cells and Ranges
Using Cut, Copy, and Paste
Using Undo and Redo
Clearing Cell Contents and Formats
Using Auto Features
Using AutoCorrect
Concepts Review
Reinforce Your Skills
Apply Your Skills
Extend Your Skills
Transfer Your Skills

LEARNING OBJECTIVES

After studying this lesson, you will be able to:

- Select, move, and copy cells and ranges
- Use Undo and Redo
- Clear cell contents, including formatting
- Complete cell entries automatically
- Use AutoCorrect effectively

In this lesson, you will expand your basic skills in Excel. You will learn various methods of editing worksheets, including replacing entries, deleting entries, and using Undo and Redo. You will also work with AutoComplete, AutoFill, and AutoCorrect. When you have finished this lesson, you will have developed the skills necessary to produce carefully edited and proofed worksheets.

Creating a Basic List in Excel

You are employed at Green Clean, a janitorial product supplier and cleaning service contractor that employs environmentally friendly practices. As the business grows, you find that organization is becoming more and more important. You decide to use Excel to create, manage, and maintain a list of employees.

	A	B	C	D	E
1	Green Clean				
2	Management and Support Roster				
3					
4	Name	Phone	Position	Employment Date	On Call
5	Tommy Choi	619-555-3224	President		
6	Mary Wright	858-555-3098	VP, Sales and Marketing	5/22/2007	Monday
7	Derek Navarro	619-555-3309	VP, Operations	3/30/2009	Tuesday
8	Isabella Riso-Neff	858-555-0211	Risk Management Director	4/13/2009	Wednesday
9	Kenneth Hazell	619-555-3224	Human Resources Director	7/17/2006	Thursday
10	D'Andre Adams	760-555-3876	Facilities Services Manager	12/7/2005	Friday
11	Talos Bouras	858-555-1002	Sales Manager	5/10/2004	Saturday
12	Michael Chowdery	858-555-0021	Purchasing Manager	10/26/2009	Sunday
13	Ahn Tran	760-555-0728	Office Manager	6/26/2006	
14	Jenna Mann	951-555-0826	Administrative Assistant	3/15/2010	
15	Nicole Romero	858-555-4987	Payroll Assistant	5/25/2009	
16	Amy Wyatt	619-555-4016	Customer Service Rep	8/17/2009	
17	Brian Simpson	858-555-3718	Customer Service Rep	12/1/2013	
18	Leisa Malimali	619-555-4017	Sales Assistant	12/1/2013	

You will use this worksheet to organize the management of key employee data.

Opening Workbooks

Video Library   http://labyrinthelab.com/videos   Video Number: EX13-V0201

The Open menu lets you navigate to any file storage location and open previously saved workbooks. Once a workbook is open, you can browse it, print it, and make editing changes. The organization and layout of the Open menu are similar to those of the Save As menu.

FROM THE RIBBON
File→Open

FROM THE KEYBOARD
Ctrl+O to open a new workbook

Excel 2013

DEVELOP YOUR SKILLS EX02-D01
Open the Workbook

In this exercise, you will open a workbook that lists various employees.

1. Start **Excel** and choose **Open Other Workbooks** to display the Open menu.

2. Click **Computer**, and then click the **Browse** button to display the Open dialog box.

3. Navigate to your file storage location (such as a USB flash drive) and double-click the **EX2013 Lesson 02** folder to open it.

4. Select **EX02-D01-Roster** and click **Open**.

To open a document, you can also double-click its filename in the Open dialog box.

Editing Entries

Video Library   http://labyrinthelab.com/videos   Video Number: EX13-V0202

You can edit the active cell by clicking in the Formula Bar and making the desired changes. You can also double-click a cell and edit the contents right there. This technique is known as in-cell editing.

Replacing Entries

Editing an entry is efficient both for long entries and for complex formulas. If the entry requires little typing, however, it is usually easier to simply retype it. If you retype an entry, the new entry will replace the previous entry.

Deleting Characters

Use the Delete and Backspace keys to edit entries in the Formula Bar and within a cell. The Delete key removes the character to the right of the insertion point, while the Backspace key removes the character to the left of the insertion point.

This is the flashing insertion point.

Tapping Backspace will remove the "A."

A ←— I —→ B

Tapping Delete will remove the "B."

DEVELOP YOUR SKILLS EX02-D02

Edit Entries

In this exercise, you will use the Formula Bar to revise the contents of cell A2, replace the contents of cell D4, and edit cell A8 directly in the cell.

1. Save your file as **EX02-D02-Roster-[FirstInitialLastName]**.

   Replace the bracketed text with your first initial and last name. For example, if your name is Bethany Smith, your filename would look like this: EX02-D02-Roster-BSmith.

2. Click **cell A2** to select it.

3. Follow these steps to edit cell A2 using the Formula Bar:

   Ⓐ Click in the **Formula Bar** just to the right of the word *List*.

   Ⓑ Tap Backspace four times to remove the word *List*, and then type **Roster**.

   Ⓒ Click the **Enter** button.

Replace an Entry

4. Click **cell D4**.

5. Type **Employment Date** and tap Enter.

   The entry Employment Date *replaces the entry* Starting Date. *Notice that the cell formatting (underlining) has been applied to the new entry.*

Use In-Cell Editing

6. Double-click **cell A8** (the cell with the name Isabella Riso).

7. Use the mouse or right arrow key → to position the flashing insertion point to the right of the last name, *Riso*.

8. Type **–Neff** and tap Enter to complete the change.

   The entry should now read Isabella Riso-Neff.

9. Click the **Save** 🖫 button to update the changes. Keep the file open.

   Clicking Save automatically saves changes to a workbook that has previously been saved.

Selecting Cells and Ranges

Video Library   http://labyrinthelab.com/videos   Video Number: EX13-V0203

To edit a worksheet (move, copy, delete, or format) you must first select the cell(s). The most efficient way to select cells is with the mouse, although you can also use the keyboard. A group of adjacent cells is called a range.

Entire columns or rows may be selected by clicking or dragging the column headings (such as A, B, C) or row headings (such as 1, 2, 3).

FROM THE KEYBOARD

Ctrl + A to select all

Ctrl + Spacebar to select a column

Shift + Spacebar to select a row

Excel Ranges

Each cell has a reference. For example, A1 refers to the first cell in a worksheet, which is at the intersection of column A and row 1. Likewise, a range reference specifies the cells included within a range. The range reference includes the first and last cells in the range, separated by a colon (:). For example, the range A4:E4 includes cells A4, B4, C4, D4 and E4.

	A	B	C	D	E
	A6		f_x	Mary Wright		
1	Green Clean				
2	Management and Support Roster				
3					
4	Name	Phone	Position	Employment Date	On Call
5	Tommy Choi	619-555-3224	President		
6	Mary Wright	858-555-3098	VP, Sales and Marketing	5/22/2007	
7	Derek Navarro	619-555-3309	VP, Operations	3/30/2009	
8	Isabella Riso-Neff	858-555-0211	Risk Management Director	4/13/2009	
9	Kenneth Hazell	619-555-3224	Human Resources Director	7/17/2006	
10	D'Andre Adams	760-555-3876	Facilities Services Manager	12/7/2005	
11	Talos Bouras	858-555-1002	Sales Manager	5/10/2004	
12	Michael Chowdery	858-555-0021	Purchasing Manager	10/26/2009	
13	Ahn Tran	760-555-0728	Office Manager	6/26/2006	
14	Jenna Mann	951-555-0826	Administrative Assistant	3/15/2010	

Range A1:A2

Range A4:E4

Range A6:D10

The selected ranges are shaded. Cell A6 is the active cell, as it is not shaded, has an outline around it, and is displayed in both the Name Box and Formula Bar.

Task	Procedure
Select a range	Drag the mouse pointer over the desired cells.
Select several ranges	Select a range; press Ctrl while selecting additional range(s).
Select an entire column	Click a column heading or press Ctrl+Spacebar.
Select an entire row	Click a row heading or press Shift+Spacebar.
Select multiple columns or rows	Drag the mouse pointer over the desired column or row headings.
Select an entire worksheet	Click the Select All ◹ button. Or, click outside the worksheet data and press Ctrl+A.
Select a range with Shift	Position the highlight in the first cell you wish to select, press Shift, and click the last cell you wish to include in your range.
Extend or decrease a selection with Shift	Press Shift while tapping an arrow key.

DEVELOP YOUR SKILLS EX02-D03

Make Selections

In this exercise, you will select multiple ranges and entire rows and columns using the mouse. You will also use Shift and Ctrl to practice selecting cell ranges.

1. Save your file as **EX02-D03-Roster-[FirstInitialLastName]**.

2. Position the **mouse pointer ✚** over **cell A4**.

3. Press and hold down the left mouse button while dragging the mouse to the right until the **range A4:E4** is selected; release the mouse button.

   Notice that for each range that is selected, the corresponding row and column headings are displayed in gray.

4. Click once anywhere in the worksheet to deselect the cells.

5. Follow these steps to select two ranges:

Ⓐ Select the **range A4:E4**.

	A	B	C	D	E
1	Green Clean				
2	Management and Support Roster				
3					
4	Name	Phone	Position	Employment Date	On Call
5	Tommy Choi	619-555-3224	President		
6	Mary Wright	858-555-3098	VP, Sales and Marketing	5/22/2007	
7	Derek Navarro	619-555-3309	VP, Operations	3/30/2009	
8	Isabella Riso-Neff	858-555-0211	Risk Management Director	4/13/2009	
9	Kenneth Hazell	619-555-3224	Human Resources Director	7/17/2006	
10	D'Andre Adams	760-555-3876	Facilities Services Manager	12/7/2005	

Ⓑ Hold down Ctrl while dragging to select the **range A6:D10**.

Ⓒ Release Ctrl after the second range is selected.

The ranges A4:E4 and A6:D10 are selected. The Ctrl key lets you select more than one range at the same time.

6. Hold down Ctrl while you select any other range, and then release Ctrl.

You should now have three ranges selected.

7. Make sure you have released Ctrl, and then click once anywhere on the worksheet to deselect the ranges.

The highlighting of the previous selections disappears.

8. Follow these steps to select various rows and columns:

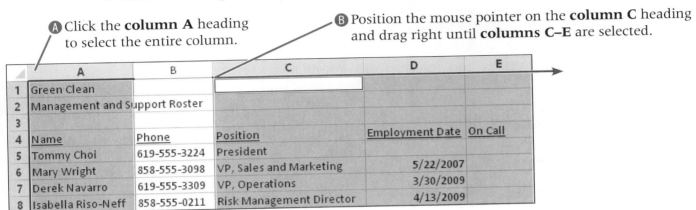

Ⓐ Click the **column A** heading to select the entire column.

Ⓑ Position the mouse pointer on the **column C** heading and drag right until **columns C–E** are selected.

Column A will be deselected because you did not hold down Ctrl.

Ⓒ Click the **Select All** button to select the entire worksheet.

Ⓓ Click the **row 1** heading to select the entire row.

Ⓔ Drag the mouse pointer down over the **row 6–10** headings.

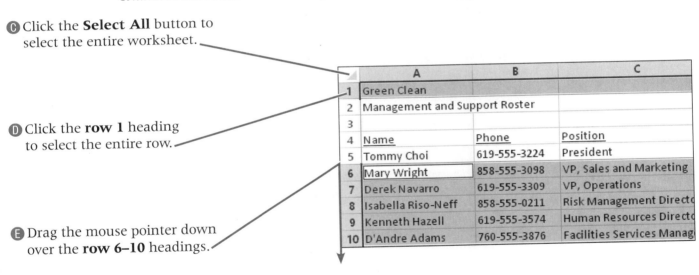

Row 1 will be deselected because you did not hold down Ctrl.

9. Follow these steps to select cells using keystrokes:

Ⓐ Click **cell A4**.

Ⓑ Hold down ⎡Shift⎤ and click **cell E16** to select the range A4:E16.

	A	B	C	D	E
4	Name	Phone	Position	Employment Date	On Call
5	Tommy Choi	619-555-3224	President		
6	Mary Wright	858-555-3098	VP, Sales and Marketing	5/22/2007	
7	Derek Navarro	619-555-3309	VP, Operations	3/30/2009	
8	Isabella Riso-Neff	858-555-0211	Risk Management Director	4/13/2009	
9	Kenneth Hazell	619-555-3224	Human Resources Director	7/17/2006	
10	D'Andre Adams	760-555-3876	Facilities Services Manager	12/7/2005	
11	Talos Bouras	858-555-1002	Sales Manager	5/10/2004	
12	Michael Chowdery	858-555-0021	Purchasing Manager	10/26/2009	
13	Ahn Tran	760-555-0728	Office Manager	6/26/2006	
14	Jenna Mann	951-555-0826	Administrative Assistant	3/15/2010	
15	Nicole Romero	858-555-4987	Payroll Assistant	5/25/2009	
16	Amy Wyatt	619-555-4016	Customer Service Rep	8/17/2009	

	A	B	C	D
12	Michael Chowdery	858-555-0021	Purchasing Manager	10/26/2009
13	Ahn Tran	760-555-0728	Office Manager	6/26/2006
14	Jenna Mann	951-555-0826	Administrative Assistant	3/15/2010
15	Nicole Romero	858-555-4987	Payroll Assistant	5/25/2009
16	Amy Wyatt	619-555-4016	Customer Service Rep	8/17/2009

Ⓒ Click **cell A12**.

Ⓓ Hold down ⎡Shift⎤ then tap →
three times and ↓ four times.

The range A12:D16 is selected. Notice that the ⎡Shift⎤ key techniques give you precise control when selecting. You should use the ⎡Shift⎤ key techniques if you find selecting with the mouse difficult or if you have a large range to select that is not entirely visible on your screen.

10. Take a few moments to practice different selection techniques; then, **Save** 🖫 the file.

Using Cut, Copy, and Paste

Video Library   http://labyrinthelab.com/videos   Video Number: EX13-V0204

You use the Cut, Copy, and Paste commands to move and copy cells. For example, use the Copy command to copy a range and the Paste command to paste it somewhere else on the same worksheet, another worksheet, or even another program. Similarly, use Cut to remove (delete) a range from one area and move it to another.

When an item is copied or cut, it is placed on the Office Clipboard. These items can then be pasted from the Clipboard, which can be opened by clicking the dialog box launcher on the Clipboard group of the Home tab.

FROM THE RIBBON
Home→Clipboard →Copy
Home→Clipboard →Cut
Home→Clipboard →Paste

FROM THE KEYBOARD
Ctrl + C to copy
Ctrl + X to cut
Ctrl + V to paste

Excel 2013

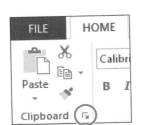

A dialog box launcher

The Office Clipboard with several items available to paste.

Paste Options

The Paste Options button displays at the lower-right corner of the destination cell(s) after a paste action. Its drop-down list provides options that let you modify the effect of the Paste command. The button disappears upon the next action you take.

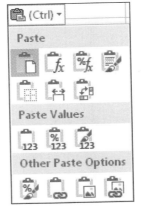

The Paste Options menu.

The Shortcut menu that appears when you right-click a cell.

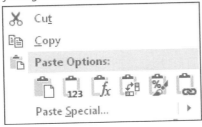

Moving and Copying Cells via Drag and Drop

Drag and drop produces the same results as Cut, Copy, and Paste. However, Drag and drop is preferable if the original location and new destination are both visible onscreen. When using drag and drop, the mouse pointer changes to a four-headed arrow as you point at the highlighted box surrounding the selected cell or range.

Moving and Copying Cells via Right-Dragging

- Move Here
- Copy Here
- Copy Here as Values Only
- Copy Here as Formats Only
- Link Here
- Create Hyperlink Here
- Shift Down and Copy
- Shift Right and Copy
- Shift Down and Move
- Shift Right and Move
- Cancel

Right-dragging is a variation of the drag-and-drop technique. With the right-drag method, the right mouse button is used to drag the selected cell or range. When the right mouse button is released, you can choose to move, copy, or link from the resulting menu (as shown here). This approach provides more control because there is no need to use Ctrl when copying. In addition, it's easy to cancel the command if you change your mind.

QUICK REFERENCE	USING CUT, COPY, AND PASTE
Task	**Procedure**
Cut a cell	Select Home→Clipboard→Cut, or right-click the cell and select Cut.
Copy a cell	Select Home→Clipboard→Copy, or right-click the cell and select Copy.
Paste a cell	Select Home→Clipboard→Paste, or right-click the cell and select Paste.
Move cells with drag and drop	Point to the dark line surrounding the selected range and drag to the desired location.
Copy cells with drag and drop	Hold Ctrl, point to the dark line surrounding the selected range, and drag to the desired location.
Move cells with right-drag and drop	Point to the dark line surrounding the selected range, right-click, and drag to the desired location.
Display the Office Clipboard	Choose Home→Clipboard→dialog box launcher.

Move and Copy Selections

In this exercise, you will use the Cut, Copy, and Paste commands as well as drag and drop to move and copy selections.

1. Save your file as **EX02-D04-Roster-[FirstInitialLastName]**.

2. Follow these steps to copy and paste a cell's contents:

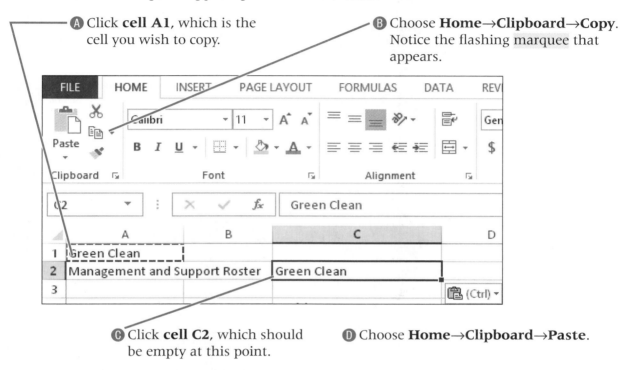

Ⓐ Click **cell A1**, which is the cell you wish to copy.

Ⓑ Choose **Home→Clipboard→Copy**. Notice the flashing marquee that appears.

Ⓒ Click **cell C2**, which should be empty at this point.

Ⓓ Choose **Home→Clipboard→Paste**.

Notice that the contents of cell A1 remain, while they now also appear in cell C2.

3. Follow these steps to cut and paste a cell's contents:

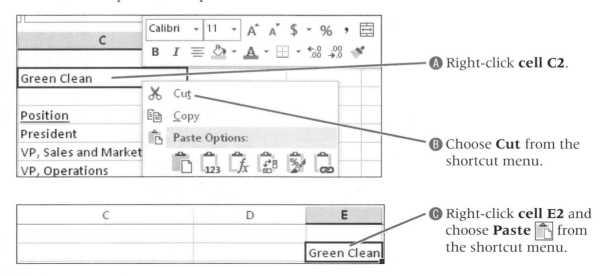

Ⓐ Right-click **cell C2**.

Ⓑ Choose **Cut** from the shortcut menu.

Ⓒ Right-click **cell E2** and choose **Paste** from the shortcut menu.

Cell C2 will now be empty because the contents were moved to cell E2.

Excel 2013

4. Follow these steps to move the contents of cell E2 via the drag-and-drop method:

Ⓐ Ensure that **cell E2** is selected.

Ⓑ Place your mouse pointer over the border of the selected cell until you see the **move pointer** ⁺ₖ.

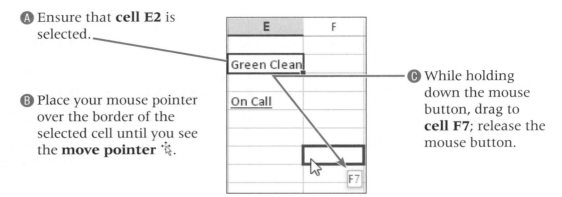

Ⓒ While holding down the mouse button, drag to **cell F7**; release the mouse button.

When you drag a cell with this method, Excel shows what cell the selection will be dropped into by displaying it on a ScreenTip, and by placing a highlight around the cell.

5. Follow these steps to copy a cell using the right-drag method:

Ⓐ Click **cell E4** and place your mouse pointer over the border of the **cell E4** until you see the **move pointer** ⁺ₖ.

Ⓑ Start dragging with the *right* mouse button. Keep the right mouse button held down.

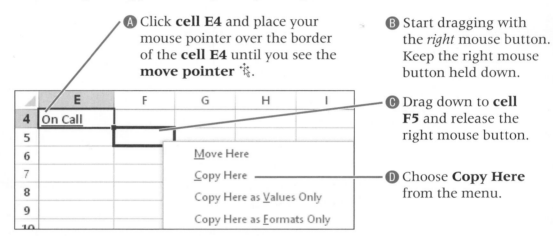

Ⓒ Drag down to **cell F5** and release the right mouse button.

Ⓓ Choose **Copy Here** from the menu.

The contents of cell E4 remain in the cell and are copied to the destination cell, F5.

6. **Save** 🖫 the workbook.

Using Undo and Redo

Video Library   http://labyrinthelab.com/videos   Video Number: EX13-V0205

The Undo button lets you reverse actions taken within a worksheet. Most actions can be undone, but those that cannot include printing and saving workbooks.

The Redo button reverses an Undo command. The Redo button will be visible on the Quick Access toolbar only after you have undone an action.

Undoing Multiple Actions

Clicking the arrow on the Undo button displays a list of actions that can be undone. You can undo multiple actions by dragging the mouse over the desired actions. You must undo actions in the order in which they appear on the drop-down list.

FROM THE KEYBOARD
Ctrl + Z to undo
Ctrl + Y to redo

Excel 2013

When you click the arrow on the Undo button, you will see a list of previous actions, with the most recent at the top.

Limitations to Undoing

In Excel, there are times when the Undo command will not work, such as when you select any command from the File tab. When an action cannot be undone, Excel will change the Undo ScreenTip to "Can't Undo."

QUICK REFERENCE	UNDOING AND REDOING ACTIONS
Task	**Procedure**
Undo the last action	▪ Click Undo ↺ on the Quick Access toolbar, or tap Ctrl + Z.
Undo a series of actions	▪ Click the drop-down arrow ↺ ˅ on the Undo button and choose the desired actions.
Redo an undone action	▪ Click Redo ↻ on the Quick Access toolbar.

Undo Actions

In this exercise, you will delete the contents of a column and use Undo to reverse the deletion. You will then use Redo to reverse an Undo command.

1. Save your file as **EX02-D05-Roster-[FirstInitialLastName]**.

2. Replace the contents of **cell C5** with **CEO**.

3. Click the **row 4** heading to select the entire row.

4. Tap Delete.

   All of the contents in row 4 are deleted.

5. Repeat **steps 3–4** for **rows 8, 12, and 14**.

Use Undo and Redo

6. Follow these steps to undo the last five commands:

   Ⓐ Click the **Undo menu** ▼ button to display a list of recent actions.

   Ⓑ Slide the mouse pointer down and choose this item.

   Excel undoes your last five commands.

7. Click **Redo** ↷ once to restore the *CEO* title in cell C5, and then click **Undo** ↶ to revert back to *President*.

8. Save the workbook.

Clearing Cell Contents and Formats

Video Library http://labyrinthelab.com/videos Video Number: EX13-V0206

In Excel, you can format cells by changing font style, size, and/or color. You can also add enhancements such as bold, italics, and underline. In this lesson, you will learn how to clear existing formatting. Clicking the Clear button displays a menu (shown here) that lets you clear content, formats, and comments from cells.

FROM THE RIBBON
Home→Editing→
Clear→Clear All

FROM THE KEYBOARD
Delete to clear cell contents

Excel 2013

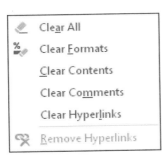

Clear All
Clear Formats
Clear Contents
Clear Comments
Clear Hyperlinks
Remove Hyperlinks

QUICK REFERENCE	CLEARING CELL CONTENTS AND FORMATTING
Task	**Procedure**
Delete cell or range contents but retain formatting	Choose Home→Editing→Clear ◢ ▾ →Clear Contents.
Delete all formatting	Choose Home→Editing→Clear ◢ ▾ →Clear Formats.
Delete comments within a cell or range of cells	Choose Home→Editing→Clear ◢ ▾ →Clear Comments.
Delete all links within a cell or range of cells	Choose Home→Editing→Clear ◢ ▾ →Clear Hyperlinks.
Delete everything	Choose Home→Editing→Clear ◢ ▾ →Clear All.

Clear Cell Contents and Formatting

In this exercise, you will use the Clear command to delete cell contents and cell formats.

1. Save your file as **EX02-D06-Roster-[FirstInitialLastName]**.

2. Click **cell F5**.

3. Choose **Home→Editing→Clear** 🧼 ▾ and then choose **Clear Formats** from the menu.

   The contents of the cell were underlined. When you choose to clear only the formats, the contents remain and the underline is removed.

4. Click **Undo** 🔄 on the Quick Access toolbar.

5. Ensure that **cell F5** is selected; then click **Clear** 🧼 ▾ and choose **Clear All**.

6. Type your name and tap Enter.

   Notice that the contents are no longer underlined in cell F5 because you cleared "all" (formatting and contents) from it.

7. Use Ctrl + Z to undo the typing of your name.

8. Click **cell F7** and tap Delete.

   The entry Green Clean *is deleted and the formatting remains in the cell.*

9. Save the workbook.

Using Auto Features

Video Library   http://labyrinthelab.com/videos   Video Number: EX13-V0207

Excel offers "auto" features that help you work more efficiently. AutoFill allows you to quickly fill a range of cells. AutoComplete makes it easy to enter long entries by typing an acronym or a series of characters, which are converted to the desired entry. AutoCorrect can also assist in correcting commonly misspelled words.

Working with AutoFill

AutoFill allows you to quickly extend a series, copy data, or copy a formula into adjacent cells by selecting cells and dragging the fill handle, which is the small black square that appears at the bottom-right corner of a selected cell or range. If the selected cell does not contain data that AutoFill recognizes as a series, the data will be copied into the adjacent cells. A black cross appears when you position the mouse pointer on the fill handle. You can drag the fill handle to fill adjacent cells to accomplish the following tasks.

- **Copy an entry:** If the entry in the active cell is a number, formula, or text entry, the fill handle copies the entry to adjacent cells.

- **Expand a repeating series of numbers:** If you select two or more cells containing numbers, Excel assumes you want to expand a repeating series. For example, if you select two cells containing the numbers 5 and 10 and drag the fill handle, Excel will fill the adjacent cells with the pattern that you have established: 15, 20, 25, etc.

- **AutoFill of date entries:** If the active cell contains any type of date entry, Excel will determine the increment of the date value and fill in the adjacent cells. For example, if the current cell contains the entry May and you drag the fill handle, AutoFill will insert the entries June, July, August, etc. in the adjacent cells.

The following table and illustrations provide examples of series that AutoFill can extend.

Excel 2013

Selected Cells	Extended Series
Mon	Tue, Wed, Thu
Monday	Tuesday, Wednesday, Thursday
Jan	Feb, Mar, Apr
January	February, March, April
Jan, Apr	Jul, Oct, Jan
1, 2	3, 4, 5, 6
100, 125	150, 175, 200
1/10/11	1/11/11, 1/12/11, 1/13/11
1/15/11, 2/15/11	3/15/11, 4/15/11, 5/15/11
1st Qtr	2nd Qtr, 3rd Qtr, 4th Qtr

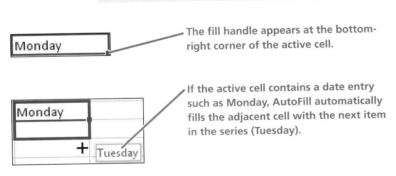

The fill handle appears at the bottom-right corner of the active cell.

If the active cell contains a date entry such as Monday, AutoFill automatically fills the adjacent cell with the next item in the series (Tuesday).

The completed series with the AutoFill Options button displayed.

AutoComplete vs. AutoFill

AutoComplete is useful when you want the same entry repeated more than once in a column. AutoFill allows you to select a cell and fill in entries by completing a series or copying the source cell, whereas AutoComplete works within a cell as you type. If the first few characters you type match another entry in the column, AutoComplete will offer to complete the entry for you. You accept the offer by tapping Tab or Enter; reject it by typing the remainder of the entry yourself.

| 16 | Amy Wyatt | 619-555-4016 | Customer Service Rep |
| 17 | Brian Simpson | 858-555-3718 | customer Service Rep |

Here, a "c" was typed and AutoComplete suggested completing the entry as *Customer Service Rep*. To accept this entry and move to the next cell, tap Tab.

AutoComplete will complete the entry "case sensitive" to match the existing entry.

DEVELOP YOUR SKILLS EX02-D07
Use AutoComplete and AutoFill

In this exercise, you will enter two new employees and use AutoComplete to speed up your work. In addition, you use AutoFill to complete a series of the days of the week.

1. Save your file as **EX02-D07-Roster-[FirstInitialLastName]**.

2. Click **cell A17**, type **Brian Simpson**, and tap Tab to move to the next cell.

3. Type **858-555-3718** and tap Tab.

4. Type **c** and notice that Excel suggests *Customer Service Rep* as the entry. Tap Tab to accept the suggestion and move one cell to the right.

   The entry is capitalized.

5. Type today's date and tap Enter.

   Notice that when you tap Enter, the highlight moves to cell A18, where you can begin typing the next list entry.

6. Type **Leisa Malimali** and tap Tab.

7. Type **619-555-4017** and tap Tab.

8. Type **S** in **cell C18**.

   Excel suggests Sales Manager *from a previous row. Leisa, however, is a sales assistant, so you need to continue typing your entry. Make sure you have typed a capital* S, *as that will not pull from the previous entries.*

9. Continue typing **ales Assistant** and tap Tab.

   Excel replaces the AutoComplete suggestion with the entry you typed, Sales Assistant.

10. Hold Ctrl and tap ʹ, then tap Enter to display today's date.

    Ctrl + ʹ copies the contents of the cell one row above the active cell.

Use AutoFill to Expand a Series

Now you will fill in the column showing the manager responsible for being on emergency call each evening.

11. Click **cell E6**.

12. Type **Monday** and click the **Enter** ✓ button.

13. Follow these steps to fill the adjacent cells:

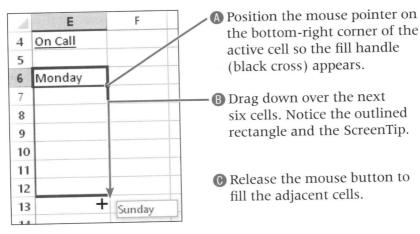

Ⓐ Position the mouse pointer on the bottom-right corner of the active cell so the fill handle (black cross) appears.

Ⓑ Drag down over the next six cells. Notice the outlined rectangle and the ScreenTip.

Ⓒ Release the mouse button to fill the adjacent cells.

14. Select **cell A1** and then save your changes.

The Auto Fill Options Button

Video Library http://labyrinthelab.com/videos Video Number: EX13-V0208

The Auto Fill Options button appears after you fill cells in a worksheet. A menu of fill options appears when you click the Auto Fill Options button.

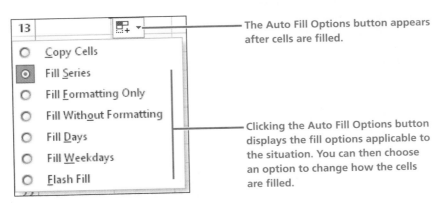

The Auto Fill Options button appears after cells are filled.

Clicking the Auto Fill Options button displays the fill options applicable to the situation. You can then choose an option to change how the cells are filled.

If you choose Fill Without Formatting, you can fill cells without copying the formatting from the original cell. Fill Formatting Only copies the formatting but not the contents from the source cells.

Use the Auto Fill Options Button

In this exercise, you will use the Auto Fill Options button to fill a data series without applying the source cell's formatting. You also will fill by applying only the formatting so that you may enter different data in cells.

1. Save your file as **EX02-D08-Roster-[FirstInitialLastName]**.

2. Choose the **Sheet2** tab at the bottom of the window, and select **cell A1**.

3. Follow these steps to AutoFill cell contents:

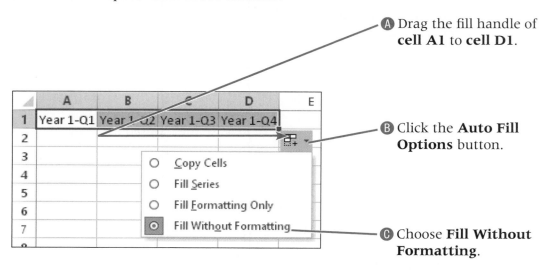

Ⓐ Drag the fill handle of **cell A1** to **cell D1**.

Ⓑ Click the **Auto Fill Options** button.

Ⓒ Choose **Fill Without Formatting**.

The formatting is removed from B1:D1.

4. Follow these steps to AutoFill formatting:

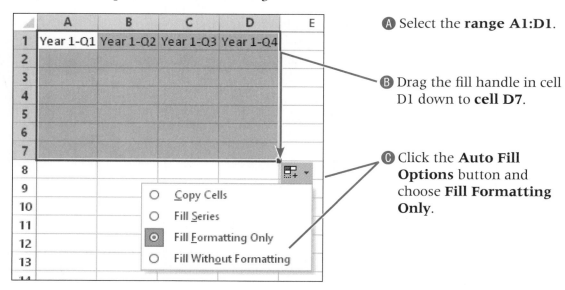

Ⓐ Select the **range A1:D1**.

Ⓑ Drag the fill handle in cell D1 down to **cell D7**.

Ⓒ Click the **Auto Fill Options** button and choose **Fill Formatting Only**.

The contents are removed from the range A2:D7, but the formatting is still applied.

5. Enter numbers shown here in the **range A2:D2**.
   Notice that the formatting matches that of the range A1:D1.

6. Select the **Sheet1** tab of the workbook; save
   the file.

	A	B	C	D
1	Year 1-Q1	Year 1-Q2	Year 1-Q3	Year 1-Q4
2	**222**	333	444	555

Using AutoCorrect

Video Library   http://labyrinthelab.com/videos   Video Number: EX13-V0209

AutoCorrect can improve the speed and accuracy of entering text. AutoCorrect is most useful for replacing abbreviations with full phrases. For example, you could set up AutoCorrect to substitute *Major League Baseball* whenever you type *mlb*. Other benefits of AutoCorrect include that it will automatically correct common misspellings (replacing "teh" with "the"), capitalize the first letter of a day (capitalizing the "s" in "sunday"), and correct words that are typed with two initial capital letters (changing the "R" to lowercase in "ORange").

AutoCorrect entries are shared by all programs in the Microsoft Office Suite, so if you've already added some in Word, they are available for you to use in Excel as well.

Expanding AutoCorrect Entries

AutoCorrect goes into action when you type a word in a text entry and tap [Spacebar], or when you complete a text entry. The word or entry is compared with all entries in the AutoCorrect table. The AutoCorrect table contains a list of words and their replacement phrases. If the word you type matches an entry in the AutoCorrect table, a phrase from the table is substituted for the word. This is known as expanding the AutoCorrect entry.

Undoing AutoCorrect Entries

There may be times that AutoCorrect replaces an entry against your wishes. AutoCorrect is treated as a single character, meaning that it is viewed by the Undo feature the same as if you typed an "a" or tapped [Delete]. Therefore, you can use Undo to reverse an AutoCorrect entry before you confirm a cell entry.

Excel 2013

Creating and Editing AutoCorrect Entries

The AutoCorrect dialog box allows you to add entries to the AutoCorrect table, delete entries from the table, and set other AutoCorrect options. To add an entry, type the desired abbreviation in the Replace box and the desired expansion for the abbreviation in the With box.

If you create the abbreviation using uppercase letters, it will not work if you type it in lowercase letters later.

QUICK REFERENCE	USING AUTOCORRECT
Task	**Procedure**
Modify AutoCorrect options	■ Choose File→Options→Proofing→AutoCorrect Options.
	■ Make desired changes; click OK twice.

Use AutoCorrect

In this exercise, you will train AutoCorrect to replace an abbreviation with a phrase and learn how to override AutoCorrect.

1. Save your file as **EX02-D09-Roster-[FirstInitialLastName]**.

2. Select **cell A1**.

3. Type **teh cat adn dog ran fast** and tap Enter.
   Notice that both of the spelling errors have been corrected by AutoCorrect.

Override an AutoCorrect Command

4. Click **cell A1**; then type **adn** and tap Spacebar.
   AutoCorrect has corrected the misspelling.

5. Use Ctrl + Z to undo the last action.
   Undo will reverse the last command, in this case AutoCorrect.

6. Tap Esc to cancel the entry.

Create an AutoCorrect Entry

7. Choose **File→Options**.

8. Follow these steps to create an AutoCorrect entry:

Ⓐ Display the **Proofing** options.   Ⓑ Choose **AutoCorrect Options**.

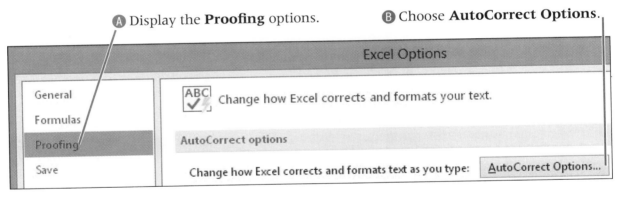

Ⓒ Type **gc** in the **Replace** box.

Ⓓ Tap Tab then type **Green Clean** in the **With** box.

Ⓔ Click **Add**.

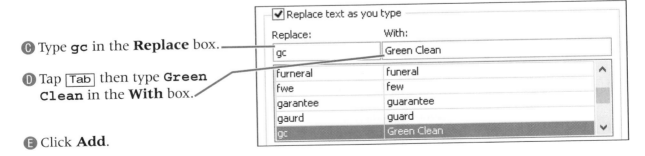

Your entry will be added to the list.

Excel 2013

9. Click **OK** in the AutoCorrect dialog box.

10. Click **OK** in the Excel Options dialog box.

Use and Delete an AutoCorrect Entry

It is important to delete the AutoCorrect entry you just created. Otherwise it will still be there when the next student uses the computer.

11. Ensure that **cell A1** is still selected; then type **gc** and tap Enter.

    The AutoCorrect entry that you created is entered into the cell.

12. Choose **File→Options** and display the **Proofing** options.

13. Choose **AutoCorrect Options**.

14. Follow these steps to delete your AutoCorrect entry:

Ⓐ Type **gc** in the **Replace** box.

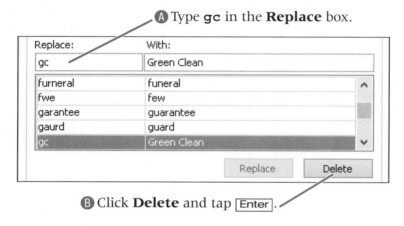

Ⓑ Click **Delete** and tap Enter.

15. Click **OK** in the Excel Options dialog box.

16. **Save** 💾 the changes and close the workbook. Exit **Excel**.

Concepts Review

To check your knowledge of the key concepts introduced in this lesson, complete the Concepts Review quiz by choosing the appropriate access option below.

If you are...	Then access the quiz by...
Using the Labyrinth Video Library	Going to http://labyrinthelab.com/videos
Using eLab	Logging in, choosing Content, and navigating to the Concepts Review quiz for this lesson
Not using the Labyrinth Video Library or eLab	Going to the student resource center for this book

Reinforce Your Skills

REINFORCE YOUR SKILLS EX02-R01

Edit a Worksheet

In this exercise, you will edit a worksheet using techniques such as cut, copy, and paste.

Edit Entries

1. Start **Excel**. Open **EX02-R01-Customers** from the **EX2013 Lesson 02** folder and save it as **EX02-R01-Customers-[FirstInitialLastName]**.

2. Select **cell B5**.

3. Type **Ralph** and tap Enter.

4. Replace the name *Calvin* in **cell B7** with the name **Stephen**.

Select Cells and Ranges

5. Select **cell D3**, drag the mouse to **cell D7**, and release the mouse button.

6. Select **cell B3**, drag the mouse to **cell F3**, and release the mouse button.
   The range D3:D7 is now deselected because you have highlighted a different range.

7. Hold Ctrl and highlight the **range B7:F7**.
   The range B3:F3 remains selected because you held down Ctrl.

8. Click the **column B** heading.
   All of column B is selected.

Work with Cut, Copy, and Paste

9. Select **cell E3**.

10. Choose **Home→Clipboard→Cut** ✂.

11. Select **cell E11** and choose **Home→Clipboard→Paste** 📋.

12. Select the **range A7:F7**; copy it using Ctrl + C.

13. Select **cell A8** and paste the **range A7:F7** using Ctrl + V.
    This approach can come in handy if you have a new entry that is very similar to an existing one!

14. Clear the contents in the **range A8:F8**.

15. Select **cell E11**.

16. Taking care to avoid the fill handle, point at the dark line surrounding the cell, press the right mouse button, and drag up to **cell E3**.
    The context menu appears when you release the mouse button.

132nd Street, Los Angeles, CA 95544

17. Choose **Move Here** from the context menu.

18. Edit the last four digits of the phone number in **cell D7** to **3535**, and confirm the change.

19. Use [Ctrl]+[Home] to return to **cell A1**.

20. Save your file then close it; exit **Excel**.

21. Submit your final file based on the guidelines provided by your instructor.

    To view examples of how your file or files should look at the end of this exercise, go to the student resource center.

Manage Cell Contents

In this exercise, you will alter the contents of a worksheet and use multiple auto features.

Use Undo and Redo

1. Start **Excel**. Open **EX02-R02-Customers2** from the **EX2013 Lesson 02** folder and save it as **EX02-R02-Customers2-[FirstInitialLastName]**.

2. Click **cell B6** and tap [Delete] to remove the cell contents.

    You realize that this data is necessary for the listing; it should not have been deleted.

3. Click **Undo** [↶] on the Quick Access toolbar.

    Notice that the cell contents have returned to cell B6. Also notice that the Redo [↷] button is now active on the Quick Access toolbar.

4. Click **Redo** [↷] to remove the cell contents once again.

    If you realized that the cell contents were incorrect, you could choose this action to remove them.

5. Type **Brenda** in **cell B6**.

Clear Cell Contents and Formats

6. Click **cell C3**.

7. Choose **Home→Editing→Clear→Clear All**.

    Both the contents and the formatting have been removed from cell C3.

8. Type **Holmes** in **cell C3**.

    Notice that the blue fill color has not returned when the new entry is typed.

Use Auto Features

9. Select **cell F7** and type **oh**.

    Notice that AutoComplete does not suggest an entry when you type "o," as there are two "o" entries in the column.

10. Tap [Tab] to accept the suggested entry of *Ohio*.

11. Select **cell A3**.

    Before using AutoFill, you must select the cell that you will be using as the basis for the fill information.

12. Place your mouse pointer over the fill handle at the bottom-right corner of the selected cell and drag down through **cell A7**. Release the mouse button when the ScreenTip shows C535.

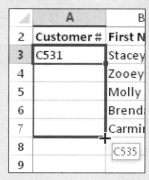

Notice that Excel recognizes C531 as the beginning of a series (C532, C533, etc.).

Use AutoCorrect

13. Choose **File→Options**.

14. Click the **Proofing** option along the left-side panel, and then click **AutoCorrect Options**.

15. In the **Replace** box, type **nc** and tap ⌜Tab⌟.

Remember to type the abbreviation in lowercase.

16. In the **With** box, type **North Carolina**.

17. Click the **Add** button; click **OK** twice.

You have now added the abbreviation for North Carolina as an AutoCorrect entry.

18. Select **cell F6**.

19. Type **nc** and tap ⌜Spacebar⌟.

The state name appears in the cell.

20. Tap ⌜Enter⌟ to confirm the entry.

21. Save your file then close it; exit **Excel**.

22. Submit your final file based on the guidelines provided by your instructor.

To view examples of how your file or files should look at the end of this exercise, go to the student resource center.

Create and Adjust a Worksheet

In this exercise, you will use various techniques to edit the contents and formatting of a worksheet.

Edit Entries

1. Start **Excel**. Open **EX02-R03-Customers3** from the **EX2013 Lesson 02** folder and save it as **EX02-R03-Customers3-[FirstInitialLastName]**.

2. Select **cell C7**.

3. Type **George** and tap ⌷Enter⌷.

4. Replace *Ross* in **cell D5** with **Taft**.

Select Cells and Ranges

5. Select **cell B3**, drag the mouse to **cell F3**, and release the mouse button.

6. Select **cell B4**, drag the mouse to **cell F4**, and release the mouse button.
   The range B3:F3 is now deselected because you have highlighted a different range.

7. Hold ⌷Ctrl⌷ and highlight the **range B6:F6**.
   The range B4:F4 remains selected because you held down ⌷Ctrl⌷.

8. Click the **row 2** heading.
   The entire row is now highlighted.

Work with Cut, Copy, and Paste

9. Select **cell F6**.

10. Choose **Home→Clipboard→Cut** ✂.

11. Select **cell F4** and choose **Home→Clipboard→Paste** 📋.

12. Use ⌷Ctrl⌷+⌷C⌷ to copy the **range B7:E7**.

13. Select **cell B8** and use ⌷Ctrl⌷+⌷V⌷ to paste the range.

14. Select the **range B8:E8**.

15. Taking care to avoid the fill handle, point at the dark line surrounding the range, press the right mouse button, and drag up to the **range B7:E7**.
    The context menu appears when you release the mouse button.

16. Choose **Move Here** from the context menu.

17. Edit the entry in **cell F3** to the correct spelling of **Minnesota** and tap ⌷Enter⌷.

18. Use ⌷Ctrl⌷+⌷Home⌷ to return to **cell A1**.

Use Undo and Redo

19. Click **cell E4** and tap Delete to remove the cell contents.

    You realize that this data is necessary for the listing; it should not have been deleted.

20. Click **Undo** ↶ on the Quick Access toolbar.

    Notice that the cell contents have returned to cell E4. Also notice that the Redo ↷ button now appears on the Quick Access toolbar.

21. Click **Redo** ↷ to remove the cell contents once again.

    If you realized that the cell contents were incorrect, you could choose this action to remove them.

22. Type **Mesa** in **cell E4**.

Clear Cell Contents and Formats

23. Click **cell D3** and choose **Home→Editing→Clear→Clear Formats**.

    The contents remain while the formatting has been removed.

Use Auto Features

24. Select **cell F7** and type **ma**.

    Notice that AutoComplete does not suggest an entry when you only type an "m," as there are two "m" entries in the column.

25. Tap Tab to accept the suggested entry of *Maine*.

26. Select **cell A3**.

    Before using AutoFill, you must select the cell that you will be using as the basis for the fill information.

27. Place your mouse pointer over the fill handle at the bottom-right corner of the selected cell and drag down through **cell A7**. Release the mouse button when the ScreenTip shows R005.

    Notice that Excel recognizes R001 as the beginning of a series (R002, R003, etc.).

Use AutoCorrect

28. Choose **File→Options**.

29. Click the **Proofing** option along the left-side menu, and then click **AutoCorrect Options**.

30. In the **Replace** box, type **wv** and tap Tab.

    Remember to type the abbreviation in lowercase.

31. In the **With** box, type **West Virginia**.

32. Click the **Add** button; click **OK** twice.

    You have now added the abbreviation for West Virginia as an AutoCorrect entry.

33. Select **cell F6**, type **wv**, and tap Spacebar.

    The state name appears in the cell.

34. Tap Enter to confirm the entry.

35. Save your file, and then close it; exit **Excel**.

36. Submit your final file based on the guidelines provided by your instructor.

Apply Your Skills

Alter Worksheet Components

In this exercise, you will use multiple techniques to edit worksheet entries and move and copy data.

Select Cells and Ranges and Edit Entries

1. Start **Excel**. Open **EX02-A01-CarpetProd** from the **EX2013 Lesson 02** folder and save it as **EX02-A01-CarpetProd-[FirstInitialLastName]**.

2. Edit the label in **cell E3** to **Price**.

3. In **cell C11**, change the entry *Granular* to **Powder**.

4. Change the entry in **cell E17** to **$4.65**.

5. Select the **range A6:E18**.

6. Drag and drop the selection so the top of it is in **row 4**.
   The selection will now be contained in the range A4:E16.

Work With Cut, Copy, and Paste

7. Select the **range B3:E3** and issue the **Cut** command.

8. Click **cell B4** and issue the **Paste** command.

9. Copy the contents of the **range B4:E4** into the **range B12:E12**.

10. Save your file, and then close it; exit **Excel**.

11. Submit your final file based on the guidelines provided by your instructor.
    To view examples of how your file or files should look at the end of this exercise, go to the student resource center.

Adjust Cell Contents

In this exercise, you will use the Undo button. You will also clear cell contents and use various auto features.

Use Undo and Redo, and Clear Cell Contents and Formats

1. Start **Excel**. Open **EX02-A02-Training** from the **EX2013 Lesson 02** folder and save it as **EX02-A02-Training-[FirstInitialLastName]**.

2. Delete the contents of **cell C4**.

3. Click the **Undo** button to bring back the cell contents.

4. Select **column C** by clicking the column header.

5. Choose **Home→Editing→Clear→Clear Formats**.

   Notice that the Medium entries remain in column C, but they are no longer formatted with borders.

Use Auto Features

6. AutoFill the ID numbers in **column B**.

7. Use **AutoComplete** to enter **print**, **audio**, and **video** in **cells C8, C9, and C10**, respectively.

8. Create an **AutoCorrect** entry of **mmm** for **Middle Management Manual**.

9. Use your **AutoCorrect** entry to quickly place **Middle Management Manual** in **cell A16**.

10. Save your file, and then close it; exit **Excel**.

11. Submit your final file based on the guidelines provided by your instructor.

    To view examples of how your file or files should look at the end of this exercise, go to the student resource center.

Make Changes to a Worksheet

In this exercise, you will use the skills you have learned in this lesson to correct an income statement.

Select Cells and Ranges and Edit Entries

1. Start **Excel**. Open **EX02-A03-IncomeState** from the **EX2013 Lesson 02** folder and save it as **EX02-A03-IncomeState-[FirstInitialLastName]**.

2. Use the Formula Bar to change the entry in **cell A12** to **Auto Expense**.

3. Replace the entry in **cell A6** with **Sales Revenue**.

4. Select the **range A16:E16**.

5. Right-drag and drop the selection so it appears in **row 15**.

Work With Cut, Copy, and Paste

6. Select the **range C5:C6** and issue the **Cut** command.

7. Click **cell D5** and issue the **Paste** command.

Use Undo and Redo and Clear Cell Contents and Formats

8. Delete the contents of **cell E4**.

9. Click the **Undo** button to bring back the cell contents.

10. Click the **Redo** button to once again delete the contents of **cell E4**.

11. Select **rows 1–3** by clicking the row headers.

12. Choose **Home→Editing→Clear→Clear Formats**.

    All formatting from the header has now been removed.

Use Auto Features

13. AutoFill the account types in **cell G6** and in the **range G10:G13**.

14. Click the **row G** header and tap ⌷Delete⌷.

15. Create an **AutoCorrect** entry of **uce** for **Universal Corporate Events**.

16. Use your **AutoCorrect** entry to quickly place **Universal Corporate Events** in **cell A2**.

17. Save your file, and then close it; exit **Excel**.

18. Submit your final file based on the guidelines provided by your instructor.

Extend Your Skills

In the course of working through the Extend Your Skills exercises, you will think critically as you use the skills taught in the lesson to complete the assigned projects. To evaluate your mastery and completion of the exercises, your instructor may use a rubric, with which more points are allotted according to performance characteristics. (The more you do, the more you earn!) Ask your instructor how your work will be evaluated.

EX02-E01 That's the Way I See It

You are known as the neighborhood Excel expert for small businesses! You are creating a worksheet for the local bank that contains information about all employees. It contains most of the necessary data, but you know that certain items were entered incorrectly by your assistant. You are now reviewing the worksheet for any incomplete entries, spelling mistakes, and formatting issues.

Open **EX02-E01-BankListing** from the **EX2013 Lesson 02** folder and save it as **EX02-E01-BankListing-[FirstInitialLastName]**.

Create an AutoComplete entry for the name of your local bank and use it to enter the name in the merged cell at the top. Review the entire worksheet. Use AutoFill to complete the missing data, use Cut and Paste where appropriate, and clear out unnecessary formatting.

You will be evaluated based on the inclusion of all elements specified, your ability to follow directions, your ability to apply newly learned skills to a real-world situation, your creativity, and the relevance of your topic and/or data choice(s). Submit your final file based on the guidelines provided by your instructor.

EX02-E02 Be Your Own Boss

Your new company Blue Jean Landscaping is doing well, and you already need a customer listing. During the first week of your business, six new customers have utilized your service.

Open **EX02-E02-BlueJeanCust** from the **EX2013 Lesson 02** folder and save it as **EX02-E02-BlueJeanCust-[FirstInitialLastName]**.

On the Data tab you will find customer information that you will need to create the listing. Using the Customer Listing tab, create the worksheet in an efficient manner, consistent with the skills you have learned in this lesson (using Copy and Paste, for one).

You will be evaluated based on inclusion of all elements specified, your ability to follow directions, your ability to apply newly learned skills to a real-world situation, your creativity, and your demonstration of an entrepreneurial spirit. Submit your final file based on the guidelines provided by your instructor.

Transfer Your Skills

In the course of working through the Transfer Your Skills exercises, you will use critical-thinking and creativity skills to complete the assigned projects using skills taught in the lesson. To evaluate your mastery and completion of the exercises, your instructor may use a rubric, with which more points are allotted according to performance characteristics. (The more you do, the more you earn!) Ask your instructor how your work will be evaluated.

EX02-T01 Use the Web as a Learning Tool

Throughout this book, you will be provided with an opportunity to use the Internet as a learning tool by completing WebQuests. According to the original creators of WebQuests, as described on their website (WebQuest.org), a WebQuest is "an inquiry-oriented activity in which most or all of the information used by learners is drawn from the web." To complete the WebQuest projects in this book, navigate to the student resource center and choose the WebQuest for the lesson on which you are currently working. The subject of each WebQuest will be relevant to the material found in the lesson.

WebQuest Subject: Altering a spreadsheet to correct formatting issues

Submit your final file(s) based on the guidelines provided by your instructor.

EX02-T02 Demonstrate Proficiency

You have decided that, based on its overwhelming popularity, you will begin to sell the Stormy BBQ secret recipe BBQ sauce across the United States. To do so, you will hire five sales representatives and will assign each to ten states. To track the new sales representatives, you will assign each a unique five-digit employee ID#, and a listing should be created that shows the employee name, employee ID#, hire date (all employees were hired on 2/1/2013), and state assignments (ensure that each representative is assigned ten states close to one another). Use the names of five of your friends for the sales representatives.

Open a blank workbook and save it as **EX02-T02-SalesReps-[FirstInitialLastName]** in your **EX2013 Lesson 02** folder. Use the concepts you have learned in this lesson to efficiently create the worksheet described above in an easily understandable format.

Submit your final file based on the guidelines provided by your instructor.

Changing the Appearance of Worksheets

LEARNING OBJECTIVES

After this lesson, you will be able to:

- Print worksheets and change workbook properties
- Insert, delete, move, copy, and rename worksheets
- Modify column width and row height
- Insert, delete, hide, and unhide columns and rows
- Set the vertical alignment and rotate text

Proper organization within an Excel workbook is, in many ways, as important as the content itself. Workbooks to be shared must be organized in a manner that allows users to quickly identify and understand the data. In this lesson, you will organize worksheet data by adjusting tab order, rows, columns, and cell alignment. You will also print worksheets and edit worksheet properties. These topics will improve your ability to organize worksheets effectively.

Changing Workbook Tabs, Columns, and Rows

Safety is a chief concern at Green Clean, a janitorial product supplier and cleaning service. You are working with the Risk Management Department to prepare company policies and procedures for legal compliance, contracts, insurance, Worker's Compensation, and workplace safety.

You will organize the structure of a workbook containing multiple worksheets. A worksheet will contain a list of learning objectives for the training topic. Test questions will be created for each objective to assess an employee's knowledge and performance regarding the objective. The worksheet will show the number of test questions in each category as well as the total and percentage score. You will work with entire rows and columns to organize the worksheet, vertically align and rotate headings, and print worksheets.

	A	B	C	D	E	F
1		Green Clean				
2		Safety Training - Chemicals				
3			Exam Categories			
4		Performance Objectives	Knowledge	Comprehension	Performance	Analysis
5			(# of Items)			
6	1.	Identify and mix hazardous materials safely.				
7	a.	Understand and follow steps on material safety data sheets (MSDS) correctly.	2	1	2	
8	b.	Identify hazardous materials		2	2	1

Column widths and row heights are adjusted to display cell contents.

24	a.	Show first aid procedures for various given incidents.		2	2	2
25	b.	Show the use of an emergency wash station.		2	2	2
26						
27						

◄ ► **Chemicals** | Lifting | Garbage | **Floors** | Notes | ⊕

Worksheet tabs are copied, rearranged, and colored to clearly identify the workbook structure.

Exploring the Many Views of Excel

Video Library http://labyrinthelab.com/videos   Video Number: EX13-V0301

Changing the view in Excel does not change how the worksheet will print. When first opened, a blank worksheet displays in Normal view. Page Layout view allows you to see how your worksheet will appear when you print it, page by page. In this view you can add headers and footers, number pages, and edit other items that print at the top and bottom of every page. In the Page Break Preview you can see blue lines representing the location of the page breaks. These lines can be dragged to any desired location. You may use either the View tab or the View buttons in the lower-right corner of the worksheet window to switch among the different worksheet views.

Zooming the View

The Zoom control lets you change the size of the onscreen worksheet but has no effect on the printed worksheet. You can zoom from 10 to 400 percent. Zooming the view can make worksheet data easier to see, and therefore facilitates worksheet editing.

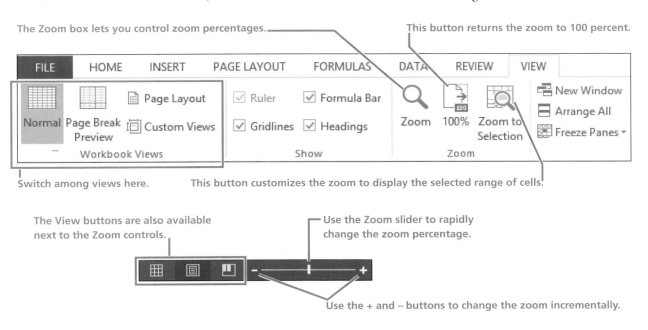

The Zoom box lets you control zoom percentages.

This button returns the zoom to 100 percent.

Switch among views here.

This button customizes the zoom to display the selected range of cells.

The View buttons are also available next to the Zoom controls.

Use the Zoom slider to rapidly change the zoom percentage.

Use the + and – buttons to change the zoom incrementally.

DEVELOP YOUR SKILLS EX03-D01
Change Views and Use the Zoom Control

In this exercise, you will change the zoom and switch between Page Layout and Normal views.

1. Start **Excel**. Open **EX03-D01-SafetyTraining** from the **EX2013 Lesson 03** folder and save it as **EX03-D01-SafetyTraining-[FirstInitialLastName]**.

   Replace the bracketed text with your first initial and last name. For example, if your name is Bethany Smith, your filename would look like this: EX03-D01-SafetyTraining-BSmith.

2. Follow these steps to adjust the zoom percentage:

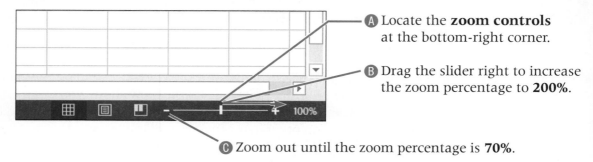

Ⓐ Locate the **zoom controls** at the bottom-right corner.

Ⓑ Drag the slider right to increase the zoom percentage to **200%**.

Ⓒ Zoom out until the zoom percentage is **70%**.

3. Select the **range A1:F5** and choose **View→Zoom→Zoom to Selection** 🔍.

   The Zoom to Selection option provides a close-up view of a selection.

4. Choose **View→Zoom→100%** 📄.

Switch between Views

5. Choose **View→Workbook Views→Page Layout View** 🔲.

   This view displays the worksheet as if printed on paper so you can check how many pages will print before printing.

6. Choose **View→Workbook Views→Normal View** ⊞.

7. Click the **Page Layout** 🔲 button, which is one of the buttons adjacent to the zoom bar at the bottom-right corner of the screen.

   The View buttons allow you to quickly toggle between views.

Check That Data Fit on One Page

8. Scroll down and to the right to view the entire worksheet.

   The gray areas will not print. They indicate which rows and columns would extend to additional printed pages if data were in them. All data in range A1:F24 fit on two pages.

9. Scroll up and to the left so **cell A1** is in view.

Edit in Page Layout View

10. Delete the contents of **cell A1**.

    You may edit the worksheet in Page Layout view just as you would in Normal view.

11. **Undo** ↺ the change.

12. Save the file and leave it open; you will modify it throughout this lesson.

    The current workbook view is saved and would reappear the next time the workbook is opened. Leave the workbook open for the next exercise.

Printing Worksheets

Video Library http://labyrinthelab.com/videos Video Number: EX13-V0302

Excel gives you several ways to print your work. These different options provide flexibility so that printing can be adapted to accommodate all workbooks.

NOTE The light gridlines displayed around cells in Normal and Page Layout views do not print.

Excel 2013

Print Preview

Print Preview shows how a worksheet will look when printed. It's always wise to preview a large or complex worksheet before sending it to the printer. The Print tab in Backstage view displays a preview along with print options. You cannot edit worksheets in Backstage view.

The Print tab

Sends the document to the printer using the print options in effect

The print preview

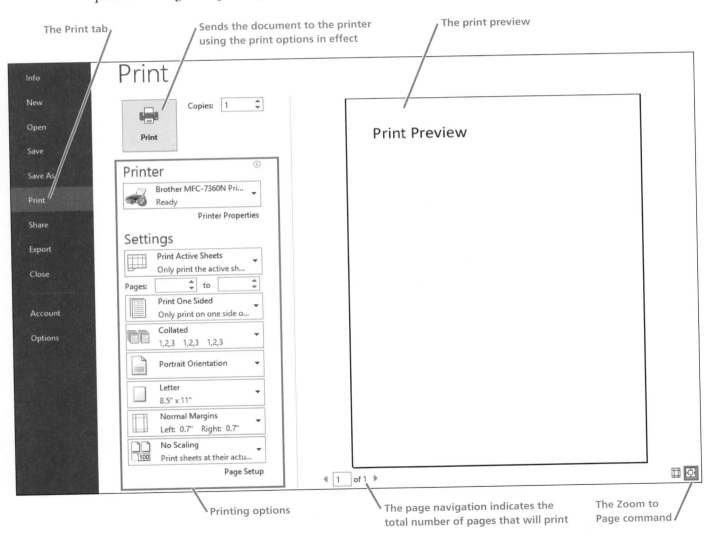

Printing options

The page navigation indicates the total number of pages that will print

The Zoom to Page command

Print the Worksheet

You can customize the Quick Access toolbar to include the Quick Print button, which sends the entire worksheet to the current printer using those print options currently in effect. You must use the Print tab in Backstage view to change printers, adjust the number of copies to be printed, print only selected cells, and more.

FROM THE RIBBON
File→Print

FROM THE KEYBOARD
Ctrl+P to print

Printing Selections

You may want to print only a single range of cells or multiple nonadjacent ranges within a worksheet. To print a selection, you must first select the desired cells. You then choose the Print Selection option in Backstage view before executing the Print command. Nonadjacent selections print on separate pages.

To print a selection, you must select the cell range before issuing the Print command.

DEVELOP YOUR SKILLS EX03-D02
Preview and Print a Worksheet

In this exercise, you will preview your worksheet in the Print tab of Backstage view, and then send it to the printer.

1. Save your file as **EX03-D02-SafetyTraining-[FirstInitialLastName]**.
2. Click the **Sheet2** tab to make that sheet active.
3. Choose **File→Print**.

   The Print tab of Backstage view opens, and a preview of page 1 displays on the right. The page navigation option at the bottom-left corner of the preview indicates that you are viewing page 1 of 1.
4. Click the **Zoom to Page** button at the lower-right corner of the preview.
5. Use the scroll bar to view the zoomed-in view.
6. Click the **Zoom to Page** button again to zoom out.
7. Review the options available at the left of the Print tab of Backstage view, and then click **Print** at the top-left corner.
8. Save the file.

Editing Workbook Properties

Video Library   http://labyrinthelab.com/videos   Video Number: EX13-V0303

Certain information about a workbook is saved along with the workbook contents. You can view these workbook properties while a workbook is open. The Windows operating system also displays document properties for a selected file.

Standard Properties

The Info tab in Backstage view displays a group of standard properties associated with Microsoft Office files. The default author name is the User Name, although you may change this if you wish. You may also enter a title, subject, categories, and comments about the workbook.

Advanced Properties

In Backstage view, you can use the Show All Properties link to display an expanded properties list. You can access two other views by displaying the Properties menu in Backstage view. Custom properties do not display in Backstage view. If you know how to use a computer programming language such as Visual Basic for Applications (VBA), you can create code using custom properties to perform additional tasks in workbooks.

Properties ˅	
Size	Not saved yet
Title	Add a title
Tags	Add a tag
Categories	Add a category
Related Dates	
Last Modified	
Created	Today, 7:37 AM
Last Printed	Today, 7:41 AM
Related People	
Author	Add an author
Last Modified By	Not saved yet
Show All Properties	

Properties ˅

Show Document Panel
Edit properties in the Document Panel above the workbook.

Advanced Properties
See more document properties

The Properties menu

QUICK REFERENCE	EDITING WORKBOOK PROPERTIES
Task	**Procedure**
Set the username	▪ Choose File→Options. ▪ Enter the desired name in the User Name box.
Edit standard properties	▪ Choose File→Info. ▪ Add or change the desired properties in Backstage view, or choose Properties menu ▼ →Show Document Panel to work with properties in the active worksheet.
Expand the Properties List	▪ Choose File→Info. ▪ Select the Show All Properties link.
Edit standard, advanced, and custom properties	▪ Choose File→Info. ▪ Choose Properties menu ▼ →Advanced Properties. ▪ Click the appropriate tab in the Properties dialog box and edit the desired items.

Edit Workbook Properties

In this exercise, you will verify the Microsoft Office username, display document properties in various ways, and set several properties.

1. Save your file as **EX03-D03-SafetyTraining-[FirstInitialLastName]**.

2. Choose **File→Options**.

   The General options category is selected by default.

3. Read the existing User Name at the bottom of the options window. (Your User Name will differ from the illustration.)

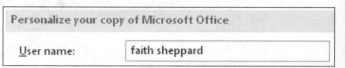

   This is the username set for all Microsoft Office documents. Do not change it unless your instructor directs you to do so.

4. Click **Cancel** to exit Excel Options.

Enter Standard Properties

5. Follow these steps to enter tags, a category, and an additional author for the workbook file:

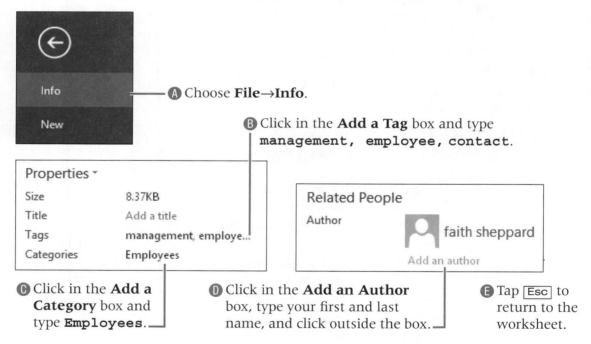

Ⓐ Choose **File→Info**.

Ⓑ Click in the **Add a Tag** box and type **management, employee, contact**.

Ⓒ Click in the **Add a Category** box and type **Employees**.

Ⓓ Click in the **Add an Author** box, type your first and last name, and click outside the box.

Ⓔ Tap Esc to return to the worksheet.

Expand the Properties

6. If necessary, choose **File→Info**.

7. Choose **Show All Properties** at the bottom-right corner of Backstage view. (Scroll down to locate the command, if necessary.)

8. Review the expanded list of properties, which include Comments, Status, and Manager.

Explore Advanced and Custom Properties

9. Click the **Properties menu** ▼ button located above the Properties list and choose **Show Document Panel**.

   After a few moments, the panel displays above the active worksheet with the properties you entered. You can also edit properties in the panel.

10. Follow these steps to explore advanced document properties:

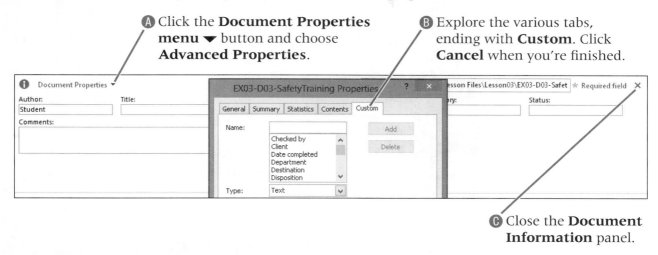

Ⓐ Click the **Document Properties menu** ▼ button and choose **Advanced Properties**.

Ⓑ Explore the various tabs, ending with **Custom**. Click **Cancel** when you're finished.

Ⓒ Close the **Document Information** panel.

A custom property may be selected or a name entered to create a new property. After the property's type and value are specified, the Add button is enabled.

11. Save the file.

Managing Worksheets

Video Library   http://labyrinthelab.com/videos   Video Number: EX13-V0304

FROM THE RIBBON
Home→Cells→Insert menu ▼→Insert Sheet

As you work with more complex workbooks, you will need to be comfortable with workbook management and worksheet navigation. You can organize a workbook by inserting, deleting, and rearranging worksheets. You also can rename worksheet tabs and apply colors to them. These options can be accessed via the Ribbon, by right-clicking, and by using keyboard controls.

FROM THE KEYBOARD
Shift + F11 to insert a worksheet

The navigation buttons

The New Sheet button inserts a new sheet to the right of the active sheet tab.

The name of the active worksheet is displayed in bold.

You cannot undo the Delete worksheet command. If you issue the command by mistake, you can close the workbook without saving and then reopen it to recover the lost worksheet.

QUICK REFERENCE	MANAGING WORKSHEETS
Task	**Procedure**
Rename a worksheet	▪ Double-click the desired worksheet tab, type a new name, and tap Enter.
Select multiple worksheets	▪ **Adjacent:** Click the first tab in the range, hold down Shift, and click the last tab in the range.
	▪ **Nonadjacent:** Click a worksheet tab, hold down Ctrl, and click additional worksheet tabs.
Change the worksheet tab color	▪ Right-click the desired sheet tab, choose Tab Color, and choose a color.
Insert a worksheet	▪ **To the right of active tab(s):** Click New Sheet.
	▪ **Before the active tab:** Choose Home→Cells→Insert menu ▼→Insert Sheet.
Insert multiple worksheets before the active sheet tab	▪ Select the desired tab, hold down Shift, and click a sheet tab at the right equal to the number of worksheets to insert.
	▪ Choose Home→Cells→Insert menu ▼→Insert Sheet.
Delete a worksheet	▪ Right-click the tab of the worksheet to delete and choose Delete.
Delete multiple worksheets	▪ Select the first worksheet tab to be deleted, hold down Ctrl, and click the other desired tab(s), or hold down Shift and select the last in a range of tabs.
	▪ Choose Home→Cells→Delete menu ▼→Delete Sheet.
Move a worksheet	▪ Drag the worksheet tab to the desired location.

DEVELOP YOUR SKILLS EX03-D04
Modify Workbook Sheet Order

In this exercise, you will insert and move a new worksheet, and delete a worksheet.

1. Save your file as **EX03-D04-SafetyTraining-[FirstInitialLastName]**.

2. Follow these steps to rename Sheet1:

    Ⓐ Double-click the **Sheet1** tab at the bottom of the worksheet to select its name.

    Ⓑ Type **Chemicals** and tap Enter. **Ⓒ** Click the **New Sheet** button twice.

    Two new sheets appear to the right of the Chemicals sheet.

3. Rename **Sheet2** as **Lifting** and rename **Sheet1** as **Notes**.

Move and Delete Sheets

4. Drag the **Lifting** sheet to the left of **Notes**.

Notice that the mouse pointer displays an empty sheet icon as you drag to the desired position, indicated by the small triangle ▼.

5. Right-click **Sheet3** and choose **Delete**.

Excel does not ask you to confirm this deletion because the worksheet is empty.

6. Click the **Lifting** sheet tab to select the sheet.

7. Hold down Shift and select the **Notes** tab.

Both tabs are now selected.

8. Choose **Home→Cells→Insert menu ▼→Insert Sheet**.

Two new sheets were inserted before the Lifting sheet. Your sheet numbers may be different.

9. Drag the **Lifting** sheet to the left of Sheet5.

10. Select the **Sheet4** tab, hold down Ctrl and select the **Sheet5** tab.

The Ctrl key allows you to select nonadjacent sheets for deletion, while the Shift key selects all sheets between the active sheet tab and the next tab you select.

11. Choose **Home→Cells→Delete menu ▼ →Delete Sheet**.

The two sheets are deleted.

12. Save the file.

Copying and Hiding Worksheets

Video Library http://labyrinthelab.com/videos   Video Number: EX13-V0305

At times it can be useful to copy a worksheet. You may want to save original data while updating the worksheet copy, or you may create a worksheet structure that can be utilized repeatedly.

Hiding and unhiding worksheets can also be useful, particularly when the end user will review only some of the worksheets. In this instance there is no benefit to showing all worksheets, and therefore hiding the unnecessary ones can create a more user-friendly workbook.

Excel 2013

QUICK REFERENCE	COPYING, HIDING, AND UNHIDING WORKSHEETS
Task	**Procedure**
Copy a worksheet	■ Select the desired sheet and hold down Ctrl while dragging its tab.
	■ When the new tab is in the desired position, release the mouse button and Ctrl.
Hide a worksheet	■ Select the desired tab and choose Home→Cells→Format→Hide & Unhide→Hide Sheet, or right-click the sheet tab and choose Hide.
Unhide a worksheet	■ Choose Home→Cells→Format→Hide & Unhide→Unhide Sheet (or right-click any sheet tab and choose Unhide); then choose the desired sheet and click OK.

Modify Workbook Sheet Tabs

In this exercise, you will copy a sheet, rename worksheet tabs, and change tab colors. You will also hide and unhide a worksheet.

Copy a Sheet

1. Save your file as **EX03-D05-SafetyTraining-[FirstInitialLastName]**.

2. Click the **Lifting** sheet tab to select the sheet.

3. Hold down Ctrl, drag the **Lifting** tab to the right to position it between Lifting and Notes, release the mouse button, and release Ctrl.

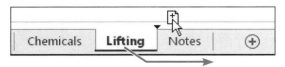

Notice that the mouse pointer displays a sheet icon containing a plus sign (+) as you drag, indicating that you are copying the sheet. The duplicated sheet is named Lifting (2).

4. Rename **Lifting (2)** to **Garbage**.

5. Repeat **steps 2–4** to copy the **Garbage** sheet and rename it as **Floors**.

6. In **cell A2** of the Floors sheet, edit *Lifting and Motion* to read **Floors**.

7. Select the **Garbage** sheet.

8. In **cell A2**, edit *Lifting and Motion* to read **Garbage**.

Change the Sheet Tab Color

9. Right-click the Chemicals sheet, point to Tab Color in the context menu, and choose the orange theme color from the palette, as shown.

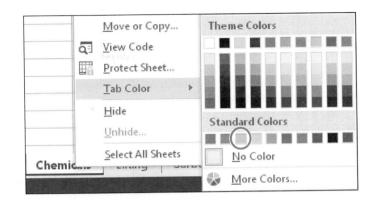

10. Repeat the above step to apply a blue theme shade to the **Lifting** sheet tab, a green theme shade to the **Garbage** sheet tab, and a purple theme shade to the **Floors** sheet tab.

    Leave the Notes tab in its original gray shade.

11. Select the **Chemicals** tab.

    Notice that the text of the currently selected tab turns bold and its color reduces to a subtle band below the text.

Hide and Unhide a Worksheet

12. Right-click the **Notes** sheet tab and choose **Hide**.

    The worksheet and its tab disappear.

13. Choose **Home→Cells→Format**.

14. Trace down to **Visibility**, point to **Hide & Unhide**, and choose **Unhide Sheet**.

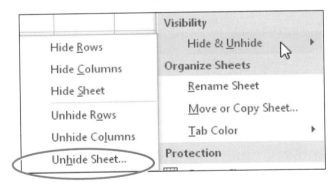

    The Unhide dialog box displays. The Notes sheet already is selected because it is the only one available to be unhidden.

15. Click **OK**.

16. Save the file.

Excel 2013

Modifying Columns and Rows

Video Library   http://labyrinthelab.com/videos   Video Number: EX13-V0306

The default column width is 8.43 characters and the default row height is 15 points. Column width and row height can be modified as desired. Strive to make data fully visible while ensuring that no unnecessary space is displayed.

There are a variety of methods for changing column width and row height. They can be performed on either one or multiple columns or rows. One efficient way to adjust widths and heights is to simply drag the column or row headings. Another method employs the AutoFit command, which adjusts to fit the widest (column) or tallest (row) entry.

	A	↔	B
1	Safety Training	- Chemicals	
2	Performance Objectives		
3			

When you point to the border between columns or rows, a double-pointed arrow appears.

QUICK REFERENCE	CHANGING COLUMN WIDTHS AND ROW HEIGHTS
Task	**Procedure**
Set a precise column width	■ Select the column, choose Home→Cells→Format→Column Width, and type the desired width.
Set column widths using AutoFit	■ **From the Ribbon:** Select the desired column(s) and choose Home→Cells→Format→AutoFit Column Width.
	■ **By double-clicking:** Select the desired column(s). Position the mouse pointer between any two selected headings (or to the right of the selected single column heading) and double-click when the double arrow mouse pointer appears.
Set a precise row height	■ Select the row, choose Home→Cells→Format→Row Height, and type the desired height.
Set row heights using AutoFit	■ Select the desired row and choose Home→Cells→Format→AutoFit Row Height. Or, select multiple rows and double-click between any two selected headings.
Manually adjust column widths and row heights	■ Select the desired column(s) or row(s) and drag (do not double-click) the heading line.

DEVELOP YOUR SKILLS EX03-D06
Change Column Width and Row Height

In this exercise, you will change the column width and row height to ensure that the cell entries fit properly.

1. Save your file as **EX03-D06-SafetyTraining-[FirstInitialLastName]**.

2. Display the **Chemicals** worksheet in **Normal** view.

3. Follow these steps to resize column A:

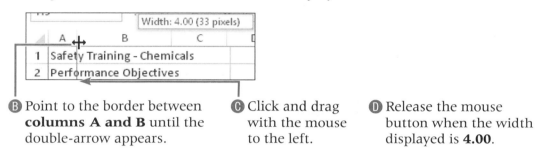 Ⓐ Place the mouse pointer here until the double-arrow mouse pointer appears, and then double-click.

Notice that the column is resized to fit the widest entry, which is in row 1. You will be merging and centering the title in row 1, so this column is too wide for your use.

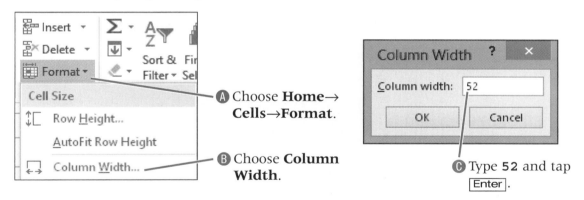

Ⓑ Point to the border between **columns A and B** until the double-arrow appears.

Ⓒ Click and drag with the mouse to the left.

Ⓓ Release the mouse button when the width displayed is **4.00**.

4. Click the **column B heading** to select the entire column.

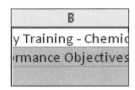

5. Follow these steps to precisely set the column width:

Ⓐ Choose **Home→ Cells→Format**.

Ⓑ Choose **Column Width**.

Ⓒ Type **52** and tap Enter.

The column now accommodates the larger cell entries, which have "spread out" because the cells are formatted to wrap text.

Use AutoFit to Adjust the Row Height

6. Click the **heading** for **row 4** and drag down through **row 24**.

Rows 4 through 24 should now be selected. Any command issued will apply to all selected rows.

7. Point between two of the selected rows to display the double-arrow pointer and double-click.

All of the selected rows shrink to fit the tallest entry. Alternatively, you can choose Home→Cells→Format→AutoFit Row Height.

8. Save the file.

Inserting and Deleting Columns, Rows, and Cells

Video Library   http://labyrinthelab.com/videos   Video Number: EX13-V0307

You can insert and delete columns, rows, and cells in your worksheets. If you want to insert or delete only cells, not entire rows or columns, you will issue a command that will prompt you to tell Excel how to shift the surrounding cells to either make room for the addition or fill the space. Depending on the format of your worksheet, this command could alter the overall structure, and should therefore be used cautiously.

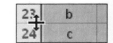

QUICK REFERENCE	INSERTING AND DELETING ROWS, COLUMNS, AND CELLS
Task	**Procedure**
Insert rows	■ Select the number of rows you wish to insert (the same number of new rows will be inserted above the selected rows). ■ Choose Home→Cells→Insert or right-click the selection and choose Insert.
Insert columns	■ Select the number of columns you wish to insert (the same number of new columns will be inserted to the left of the selected columns). ■ Choose Home→Cells→Insert or right-click the selection and choose Insert.
Delete rows	■ Select the rows you wish to delete. ■ Choose Home→Cells→Delete or right-click the selection and choose Delete.
Delete columns	■ Select the columns you wish to delete. ■ Choose Home→Cells→Delete or right-click the selection and choose Delete.
Insert cells	■ Select the cells in the worksheet where you want the inserted cells to appear. ■ Choose Home→Cells→Insert or right-click the selection, choose Insert, and then choose the desired Shift Cells option.
Delete cells	■ Select the cells you wish to delete. ■ Choose Home→Cells→Delete or right-click the selection, choose Delete, and then choose the desired Shift Cells option.

Add and Remove Rows, Columns, and Cells

In this exercise, you will insert and delete rows, as well as insert cells into the worksheet.

1. Save your file as **EX03-D07-SafetyTraining-[FirstInitialLastName]**.

2. On the **Chemicals** worksheet, use the [Ctrl] key to select **rows 15 and 24**.

   The rows in which there are no objectives listed are now selected.

3. With both rows still selected, right-click **row 24** and choose **Delete**.

   The data below a deleted row moves up.

Add Another Row to the Sheet

4. Select **row 6**.

   When you choose to insert a row, the new row will be placed above the row you have selected.

5. Click the **Insert** ⊞ button (not the menu ▼ button) and enter the text shown in the appropriate cells.

◢	A	B		C	D	E	F
6	b.	Identify hazardous materials.			2	2	1

Insert Cells into the Worksheet

To merge and center the contents of cell A1 over the entire worksheet, you need to "bump" everything in columns C through F down one row.

6. Select the **range C1:F1**.

7. Follow these steps to insert the cells and shift your existing data down:

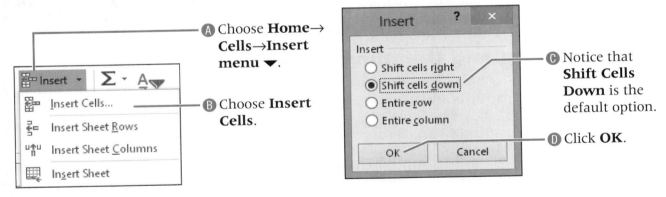

Ⓐ Choose **Home→Cells→Insert menu ▼**.

Ⓑ Choose **Insert Cells**.

Ⓒ Notice that **Shift Cells Down** is the default option.

Ⓓ Click **OK**.

8. Select the **range A3:B3** and choose **Home→Cells→Insert** ⊞.

   Everything in columns A and B, below cells A3 and B3, is shifted down one cell.

9. Select **row 1** and choose **Home→Cells→Insert** ⊞ again.

   Because you selected an entire row first, a new row is inserted. You will now apply some formatting to make the worksheet more presentable.

Excel 2013

10. Follow these steps to merge and center a range:
    - Select the **range A1:F1**.
    - Choose **Home→Alignment→Merge & Center** 🔳.
    - While the merged range is still selected, choose Home→Font→Font Size→**16**.
    - Type `Green Clean` in the merged cell.

    The font size was applied to Green Clean *even though this formatting was changed before you typed the title.*

11. **Merge & Center** 🔳 the **range A2:F2** and change the font size to **14**.

12. **Merge & Center** 🔳 the **range A3:B5** and change the font size to **14**.

    Notice that the Merge & Center command works to merge both columns and rows at once.

13. **Merge & Center** 🔳 the **range C3:F3** and choose Home→Font→Bottom Border.

14. **Merge & Center** 🔳 the **range C5:F5**.

15. Save the file.

Formatting and Hiding Columns and Rows

Video Library   http://labyrinthelab.com/videos   Video Number: EX13-V0308

You can format, hide, and unhide columns and rows by first selecting the desired columns or rows. You can make your selection in several ways: clicking a single column or row heading, dragging to select adjacent headings, or holding Ctrl while you click each nonadjacent heading. Once you have selected the desired rows or columns, apply formatting just as you would to a single cell or range. The formatting is applied to every cell across the row or down the column to the end of the worksheet.

Hiding and Unhiding Columns and Rows

There may be times when you wish to hide certain rows or columns from view (such as when you distribute a worksheet to a user who is not interested in certain worksheet details). The hidden rows and columns will not be visible, nor will they print, but they will remain part of the worksheet. After rows or columns have been hidden, you can use Unhide to make them visible again.

	A	B	C	E
2		Safety Training - Chemicals		

Notice that column D and row 1 are not visible once the Hide command is issued.

Task	Procedure
Hide columns or rows	▪ Select the desired column(s) or row(s) and choose Home→Cells→Format→Hide & Unhide→Hide Columns or Hide Rows. Or, right-click the column heading and choose Hide.
Unhide columns or rows	▪ Select the columns to the left/right or rows above/below the column(s)/row(s) you wish to unhide. Drag up from row 2 or left from column B if unhiding row 1 or column A.
	▪ Choose Home→Cells→Format→Hide & Unhide→Unhide Columns or Unhide Rows. Or, right-click the column heading and choose Unhide.

Excel 2013

DEVELOP YOUR SKILLS EX03-D08
Hide and Unhide Columns and Rows

In this exercise, you will hide and unhide rows and columns.

1. Save your file as **EX03-D08-SafetyTraining-[FirstInitialLastName]**.

2. If necessary, select the **Chemicals** worksheet.

3. Follow these steps to hide columns C–D:

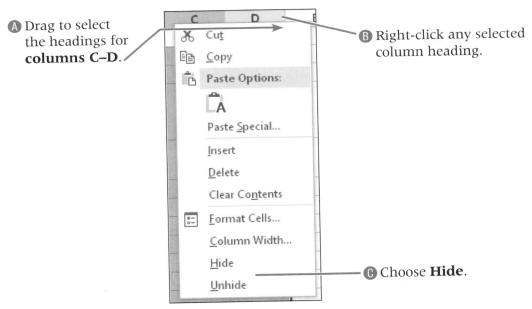

Ⓐ Drag to select the headings for **columns C–D**.

Ⓑ Right-click any selected column heading.

Ⓒ Choose **Hide**.

Columns C and D are no longer visible.

4. Right-click the **row 1** heading and choose **Hide**.

5. Follow these steps to unhide columns C–D:

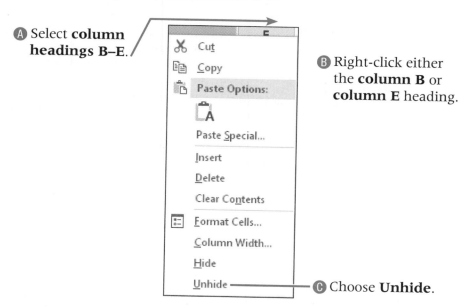

Ⓐ Select **column headings B–E**.

Ⓑ Right-click either the **column B** or **column E** heading.

Ⓒ Choose **Unhide**.

6. Follow these steps to unhide row 1:

Ⓐ Select from **row heading 2** up to the **Select All** button.

Ⓑ Right-click the **row heading 2**.

Ⓒ Choose **Unhide**.

7. Save the file.

Changing Vertical Alignment and Rotating Text

Video Library   http://labyrinthelab.com/videos   Video Number: EX13-V0309

Vertical alignment positions cell contents between the top and bottom of the cell. Options include top, bottom, center, and justify; the default alignment is bottom. Justified alignment evenly distributes unused space between lines in a multiple-line entry so text fills the cell from the top edge to the bottom edge. Justify can only be selected via the Alignment dialog box launcher button.

Rotating Text

The Orientation option has several rotation options that you can apply to text in a cell. Excel increases the row height to accommodate the rotated text. While rotating text can make titles more aesthetically pleasing, be certain that the rotation does not increase row height such that worksheet data becomes difficult to view.

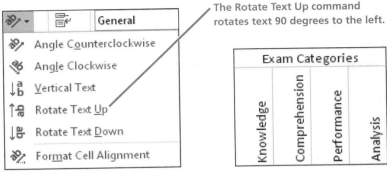

The Rotate Text Up command rotates text 90 degrees to the left.

Orienting the column headings vertically makes the column widths narrower.

QUICK REFERENCE	SETTING VERTICAL ALIGNMENT AND TEXT ROTATION
Task	**Procedure**
Set cell content to align vertically	■ Select the desired cell(s) and choose Home→Alignment→Top Align, Middle Align, or Bottom Align.
Set cell content to justify vertically within a cell	■ Select the desired cell(s), choose Home→Alignment dialog box launcher, click the Vertical drop-down arrow under Text Alignment, and choose Justify.
Rotate text within a cell using a preset option	■ Select the desired cell(s), choose Home→Alignment→Orientation, and select the desired preset.
Rotate text within a cell using a precise number of degrees	■ Select the desired cell(s), choose Home→Alignment dialog box launcher, and choose the desired text rotation.

DEVELOP YOUR SKILLS EX03-D09

Rotate Text and Change Its Vertical Alignment

In this exercise, you will rotate the categories at the top of the worksheet as well as change the vertical alignment in cells.

1. Save your file as **EX03-D09-SafetyTraining-[FirstInitialLastName]**.

2. Select the **range C4:F4** and choose **Home→Alignment→Orientation** ⧉ ▾ →**Rotate Text Up**.

   The headings are rotated in their cells. Normally, the row height would increase automatically to AutoFit the headings. In this case, the merged text in row 3 prevented that from happening.

3. Point at the bottom of the **row 4 header** until the double-arrow pointer displays, and then double-click.

   The row height increases so that all rotated text is visible.

4. Follow these steps to AutoFit columns C–F:

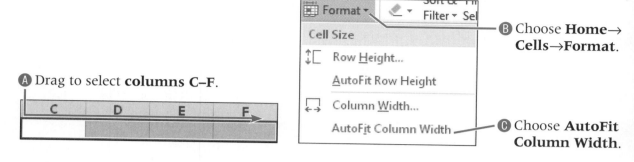

Ⓐ Drag to select **columns C–F**.

Ⓑ Choose **Home→ Cells→Format**.

Ⓒ Choose **AutoFit Column Width**.

Change Vertical Alignment

5. Select **cell A3** and choose **Home→Alignment→Middle Align** ☰.

6. Select the **range A6:F25** and choose **Home→Alignment→Top Align** ☰.

   The data now aligns at the top of cells. You have decided that the alphabet letters in column A should be aligned at the right of their cells.

7. Select the **range A7:A10**, and choose **Home→Alignment→Align Right** ☰.

8. Choose Home→Clipboard→Format Painter, and select the range A12:A14 to copy the formatting from the range A7:A10. Repeat this process for the ranges A16:A17, A19:A22, and A24:A25.

9. Save and then close the file; exit **Excel**.

Concepts Review

To check your knowledge of the key concepts introduced in this lesson, complete the Concepts Review quiz by choosing the appropriate access option below.

If you are...	Then access the quiz by...
Using the Labyrinth Video Library	Going to http://labyrinthelab.com/videos
Using eLab	Logging in, choosing Content, and navigating to the Concepts Review quiz for this lesson
Not using the Labyrinth Video Library or eLab	Going to the student resource center for this book

Reinforce Your Skills

Preview, Print, and Manage a Worksheet

In this exercise, you will preview and then print a selection from a workbook. You will also alter workbook tags and insert a new worksheet.

Explore the Many Views of Excel

1. Start **Excel**. Open **EX3-R01-Birthdays** from the **EX2013 Lesson 03** folder and save it as `EX03-R01-Birthdays-[FirstInitialLastName]`.

2. Click the **Page Layout** button on the status bar at the left of the zoom slider.

   The worksheet contents fit on a single page.

3. Check the overall look of data on the page.

   Here you confirm that the printed page will have a logical appearance.

Print Worksheets

4. Choose **File→Print**.

   A preview displays at the right of the Print tab in Backstage view.

5. Take a moment to look at the print options but do not change them.

6. Tap [Esc] to cancel printing and return to Page Layout view.

7. Click the **Normal View** ⊞ button on the status bar.

   You will print just the birthdays for the first half of the year in the next steps. You could have selected the range in Page Layout view.

8. Select the **range A1:B7**.

9. Use [Ctrl] + [P] to display the Print tab in Backstage view.

10. Review the selected printer and ensure that it is correct.

    If directed by your instructor, print to a PDF file in this step.

11. Click **Print Active Sheets**, choose **Print Selection**, and click **Print**.

    Only the selected range prints.

12. Use [Ctrl] + [Home] to go to **cell A1**.

Edit a Workbook Property

13. Choose **File→Info** to enter Backstage view.

14. Enter the keywords **employees, birthday** in the Tags box.

15. Click the **Back** arrow to exit Backstage view.

Manage Worksheets

16. Double-click the **Sheet1** tab and rename it **Finance**.

17. Click the **New Sheet** button to create **Sheet1**.

18. Double-click the **Sheet1** tab and rename it **Marketing**.

    The tabs now represent individual departments within Kids for Change.

19. Right-click the **Marketing** tab and select a **Blue** tab color.

20. Save the file and then close it; exit **Excel**.

21. Submit your final file based on the guidelines provided by your instructor.

    To view examples of how your file or files should look at the end of this exercise, go to the student resource center.

REINFORCE YOUR SKILLS EX03-R02

Adjust Columns and Rows, and Align Text

In this exercise, you will modify a donation worksheet by removing, inserting, and modifying line items. You will also hide a column and alter text alignment.

Modify Columns and Rows

1. Start **Excel**. Open **EX03-R02-DonationForm** from the **EX2013 Lesson 03** folder and save it as **EX03-R02-DonationForm-[FirstInitialLastName]**.

2. Point at the border to the right of the **column A heading** until the pointer displays a two-headed arrow and then double-click.

   You have now AutoFit Column A, and can read the names of each donating corporation.

3. Select **column B** by clicking the column heading.

4. Choose **Home→Cells→Format→Column Width**, enter a width of **10**, and click **OK**.

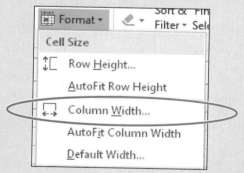

Insert and Delete Columns, Rows, and Cells

5. Select **row 3** by clicking the row heading.

6. Choose **Home→Cells→Delete** (taking care not to click the menu ▼ button).

7. Select **row 7** by clicking the row heading.

8. Choose **Home→Cells→Insert**.

9. Choose **Home→Cells→Format→Row Height**, enter a height of **6**, and click OK.
   These row adjustments have created more logical spacing throughout the worksheet.

Hide Columns and Rows

10. Select **row 15**.

11. Choose **Home→Cells→Format→Hide & Unhide→Hide Rows**.
    The thank-you message in row 15 is now hidden from view.

12. Select **rows 14 and 16**.
    The header for both rows must be selected in order to unhide row 15.

13. Choose **Home→Cells→Format→Hide & Unhide→Unhide Rows**.

Change Vertical Alignment and Rotate Text

14. Highlight **cells A6:B6**.

15. Choose **Home→Alignment→Orientation** →**Angle Counterclockwise**.
    The column titles within the cells now stand out from the text below.

16. Save the file and then close it; exit **Excel**.

17. Submit your final file based on the guidelines provided by your instructor.
    To view examples of how your file or files should look at the end of this exercise, go to the student resource center.

REINFORCE YOUR SKILLS EX03-R03

Change the Overall Worksheet Appearance

In this exercise, you will preview and then print the workbook. You will also alter workbook tags, insert a new worksheet, and adjust rows and columns.

Explore the Many Views of Excel

1. Start **Excel**. Open **EX03-R03-Partners** from the **EX2013 Lesson 03** folder and save it as `EX03-R03-Partners-[FirstInitialLastName]`.

2. Click the **Page Break Preview** button on the status bar at the left of the zoom slider.
   The blue line, representing a page break, is shown below row 9.

3. Drag the page break between **rows 15 and 16**.
   Because the print area ends at row 15, dragging the page break here will make it disappear.

Print Worksheets

4. Choose **File→Print**.

   A preview displays at the right of the Print tab in Backstage view.

5. Take a moment to look at the print options but do not change them.

6. Tap Esc to cancel the print and return to Page Break Preview.

7. Click the **Normal View** ⊞ button on the status bar.

   You will print the worksheet now so you can compare it with the completed worksheet that is produced at the end of the exercise.

8. Use Ctrl + P to display the Print tab of Backstage view.

9. Make certain that the selected printer is correct, and then click the **Print** button.

   If directed by your instructor, print to a PDF file in this step.

10. Use Ctrl + Home to go to cell A1.

Edit a Workbook Property

11. Choose **File→Info** to enter Backstage view.

12. Enter the keywords `partnership, cleanup` in the Tags box under **Properties** at the right of Backstage view.

13. Enter the Title `Partnership Organizations` in the Title box under **Properties** at the right of Backstage view.

14. Click the **Back** arrow to exit Backstage view.

Manage Worksheets

15. Hold down Ctrl and drag the **Sheet1** tab to the right.

    A copy of the Sheet1 tab has been created. This copy can be used to create a Partnership Form for a different program.

16. Double-click the **Sheet1** tab and rename it `Environmental`.

17. Double-click the **Sheet1 (2)** tab and rename it `Tutoring`.

    The tabs now represent two different programs within Kids for Change. You will modify only the Environmental tab in order to improve the appearance.

Modify Columns and Rows

18. With the Environmental worksheet selected, point at the border to the right of the **column A heading** until the pointer displays a two-headed arrow and double-click.

    You have now AutoFit Column A, however the width of the title in cell A2 causes the column to be too wide.

19. Point at the border to the right of the **column A heading**, and drag to the left so that the width equals 26 characters.

20. Select **column B** by clicking the column heading.

21. Choose **Home→Cells→Format→Column Width**, enter a width of 14, and click OK.

22. Select **row 1** by clicking the row heading.

23. Double-click the border between the headers for **row 1 and 2**.
    You have now AutoFit Row 1, and can read the company name.

Insert and Delete Columns, Rows, and Cells

24. Right-click the **row 3 heading** and choose **Delete**.

25. Right-click the **row 7 heading** and choose **Insert**.
    The new spacing gives the worksheet a better overall appearance.

Hide Columns and Rows

26. Right-click the **row 15 heading** and choose **Hide**.
    The note in row 15 is now hidden from view.

27. Select **rows 14 and 16**.
    The header for both rows must be selected in order to unhide row 15.

28. Right-click either of the selected rows, and choose **Unhide**.
    You decide that the worksheet looked better with the note hidden.

29. Click the **Undo** ⤺ button to again hide row 15.

Change Vertical Alignment and Rotate Text

30. Highlight **cells A6:C6** and choose **Home→Alignment→Orientation** 🖉▾ **→Angle Counterclockwise**.
    The column titles within the cells now stand out from the text below.

31. Save the file and then close it; exit **Excel**.

32. Submit your final file based on the guidelines provided by your instructor.

Apply Your Skills

Use Page Layout View; Edit and Manage a Workbook

In this exercise, you will adjust elements of a workbook and will review the print preview.

Explore the Many Views of Excel and Print Worksheets

1. Start **Excel**. Open **EX03-A01-Bonuses** from the **EX2013 Lesson 03** folder and save it as **EX03-A01-Bonuses-[FirstInitialLastName]**.

2. View the worksheet in **Page Layout**  view.

3. Edit the label in **cell A2** to read **Site Safety Bonuses**.

4. Enter **Backstage view** for the worksheet.

5. Check the preview on the **Print** tab to make certain the worksheet will print on one page.

6. Exit **Backstage view** without printing.

Edit Workbook Properties and Manage Worksheets

7. Add a **Category** workbook property that is appropriate for this worksheet.

8. Change the **Title** workbook property to **Bonuses**.

9. View the worksheet in **Normal** view.

10. Change the names of the worksheet tabs to indicate which half of the year is contained within each.

11. Hide the worksheet tab for the first half of the year.
    As this is not the current tab, hiding it will reduce clutter within the workbook.

12. Save the file and then close it; exit **Excel**.

13. Submit your final file based on the guidelines provided by your instructor.
    To view examples of how your file or files should look at the end of this exercise, go to the student resource center.

APPLY YOUR SKILLS EX03-A02

Restructure a Report

In this exercise, you will alter column and row widths, adjust and hide rows, and change the vertical alignment of the header.

Modify Columns and Rows

1. Start **Excel**. Open **EX03-A02-AcctsRec** from the **EX2013 Lesson 03** folder and save it as **EX03-A02-AcctsRec-[FirstInitialLastName]**.

2. Increase the row height of **rows 7–13** to add some extra space among the entries.
   For a more consistent presentation, ensure that these rows all have the same row height.

3. Increase the row height of **row 1** to 36.

4. AutoFit **column C** and widen **column A** to ensure that all entries can be read and that no column is unnecessarily wide.

Insert, Delete, and Hide Columns, Rows, and Cells

5. Delete the empty cells in **rows 5 and 8**.

6. Insert a new column after **column A**, and reduce the width to **2**.

7. Hide **rows 2 and 4** so the report name and date are not shown.
   After doing so, you realize that the report name should remain within the worksheet.

8. Unhide **row 2** so that the report name reappears.

Change Vertical Alignment and Rotate Text

9. **Middle Align** ☰ the title in **cell A1**.

10. **Top Align** ☰ the contents of **rows 6–11**.

11. Save the file and then close it; exit **Excel**.

12. Submit your final file based on the guidelines provided by your instructor.
    To view examples of how your file or files should look at the end of this exercise, go to the student resource center.

APPLY YOUR SKILLS EX03-A03

View, Print, and Restructure a Report

In this exercise, you will correct the structure of an accounts payable report.

Explore the Many Views of Excel and Print Worksheets

1. Start **Excel**. Open **EX03-A03-AcctsPay** from the **EX2013 Lesson 03** folder and save it as **EX03-A03-AcctsPay-[FirstInitialLastName]**.

2. View the worksheet in **Page Break Preview** 🔲.

3. Adjust the page break so all contents fit within one page.

4. Enter **Backstage view** for the worksheet.

5. Check the Print Preview on the **Print** tab to confirm that the page break has been removed.

6. Exit **Backstage view** without printing.

Edit Workbook Properties and Manage Worksheets

7. Add an **Author** workbook property in the **Related People** section of the Info tab in Backstage view. Use your first and last name for the new author name.

8. Change the **Tags** workbook property to **Payables**.

9. View the worksheet in **Normal** ▦ view.

10. Change the name of the worksheet tab to indicate the content of the worksheet.

Modify, Insert, Delete, and Hide Columns, Rows, and Cells

11. Set the row height of **rows 7–13** to **18**.

12. Increase the row height of **row 1** to **36**.

13. AutoFit **column C** and widen **column A** to ensure that all entries can be read and that no column is unnecessarily wide.

14. Delete the empty cells in **rows 4 and 10**.

15. Insert a new column before **column B**, and reduce the width to **2**.

16. Hide **rows 1 and 4** so the company name and date are not shown.
    After doing so, you realize that the company name should remain within the worksheet.

17. Unhide **row 1** so that the company name reappears.

18. Delete the contents of **cell C3**.

Change Vertical Alignment and Rotate Text

19. **Top Align** ☰ the title in cell A1.

20. **Middle Align** ☰ the contents within rows 6:11.

21. Save the file and then close it; exit **Excel**.

22. Submit your final file based on the guidelines provided by your instructor.

Extend Your Skills

In the course of working through the Extend Your Skills exercises, you will think critically as you use the skills taught in the lesson to complete the assigned projects. To evaluate your mastery and completion of the exercises, your instructor may use a rubric, with which more points are allotted according to performance characteristics. (The more you do, the more you earn!) Ask your instructor how your work will be evaluated.

EX03-E01 That's the Way I See It

You are known as the neighborhood Excel expert for small businesses! In this exercise, you will create a worksheet that includes three different lists of your favorite local restaurants, retail stores, and movie theaters for inclusion in the local online newspaper.

For each list include five locations (you may want to use the Internet to identify suitable entries), as well as the associated address and phone number. Remember to include a heading at the top of the worksheet, properly name the worksheet tab, and include appropriate spacing throughout. Also ensure that the spreadsheet's appearance, when printed, will be logically structured and easy to understand. Save your file as **EX03-E01-FavoritesList-[FirstInitialLastName]** in the **EX2013 Lesson 03** folder.

You will be evaluated based on the inclusion of all elements specified, your ability to follow directions, your ability to apply newly learned skills to a real-world situation, your creativity, and the relevance of your topic and/or data choice(s). Submit your final file based on the guidelines provided by your instructor.

EX03-E02 Be Your Own Boss

In this exercise, you will create and format a pair of pricing sheets for your company, Blue Jean Landscaping. These pricing sheets will be used to estimate the total cost of a job based on the services that are requested. Create a new workbook named **EX03-E02-PricingSheets-[FirstInitialLastName]** in the **EX2013 Lesson 03** folder.

Create two worksheets, one listing the price of five different landscaping services that can be provided and another listing the price of five different types of greenery that can be planted. Within the greenery listing, create columns to allow for at least two different sizes of each plant. Be sure to appropriately name each tab, include a proper heading within each worksheet, and ensure that the printed sheet will have a logical appearance by both modifying columns and rows and by using vertical alignment and text rotation.

You will be evaluated based on the inclusion of all elements specified, your ability to follow directions, your ability to apply newly learned skills to a real-world situation, your creativity, and your demonstration of an entrepreneurial spirit. Submit your final file based on the guidelines provided by your instructor.

Transfer Your Skills

In the course of working through the Transfer Your Skills exercises, you will use critical-thinking and creativity skills to complete the assigned projects using skills taught in the lesson. To evaluate your mastery and completion of the exercises, your instructor may use a rubric, with which more points are allotted according to performance characteristics. (The more you do, the more you earn!) Ask your instructor how your work will be evaluated.

EX03-T01 Use the Web as a Learning Tool

Throughout this book, you will be provided with an opportunity to use the Internet as a learning tool by completing WebQuests. According to the original creators of WebQuests, as described on their website (WebQuest.org), a WebQuest is "an inquiry-oriented activity in which most or all of the information used by learners is drawn from the web." To complete the WebQuest projects in this book, navigate to the student resource center and choose the WebQuest for the lesson on which you are currently working. The subject of each WebQuest will be relevant to the material found in the lesson.

WebQuest Subject: Researching restaurant suppliers and creating a corresponding supplier listing

Submit your final file(s) based on the guidelines provided by your instructor.

EX03-T02 Demonstrate Proficiency

You have been maintaining a workbook listing ingredients used in the dishes served at Stormy BBQ. Within the workbook you have one worksheet for lunch ingredients and one worksheet for dinner ingredients. As you have been busy running the restaurant, you have not yet taken the time to modify the columns and rows in the worksheet so that it is structured in a logical manner.

Open **EX03-T02-Ingredients** from the **EX2013 Lesson 03** folder and save it as **EX03-T02-Ingredients-[FirstInitialLastName]**. Using the techniques you have learned in this lesson, include titles and proper spacing throughout both worksheets, utilize different vertical alignment and rotation settings, and name each worksheet appropriately. Ensure that the file will be easy to read when printed, and then print a file for your instructor or create a PDF file.

Submit your final file based on the guidelines provided by your instructor.

EXCEL 2013

Working with Formulas and Functions

In this lesson, you will create and modify basic formulas and functions in Excel. Formulas are one of Excel's most powerful features, as they can save you time and increase the accuracy of your spreadsheets. You will reference cells in formulas and use AutoSum. Lastly, you will use IF functions, which can flag a cell with a text label, display a value, or perform a calculation when specific criteria are satisfied.

LESSON OUTLINE

Working with Formulas and Functions
Creating Formulas
Using Cell References in Formulas
Modifying and Copying Formulas
Displaying and Printing Formulas
Using Formula AutoComplete
Using Insert Function
Creating Formulas with the IF Function
Concepts Review
Reinforce Your Skills
Apply Your Skills
Extend Your Skills
Transfer Your Skills

LEARNING OBJECTIVES

After studying this lesson, you will be able to:

- Create formulas to calculate values
- Use functions such as sum, average, maximum, minimum, and IF
- Use relative, absolute, and mixed cell references in formulas
- Modify and copy formulas
- Display formulas rather than resulting values in cells

Creating a Spreadsheet with Formulas

Green Clean earns revenue by selling janitorial products and contracts for cleaning services. You want to set up a workbook with two worksheets, one to track commissions and the other to report how the projected profit would change based on costs and an increase or decrease in sales.

	A	B	C	D	E	F	G
1	**Sales Department**						
2	*First Quarter Commissions*						
3							
4	*Sales Team Member*	*January*	*February*	*March*	*Qtr 1 Total*	*Sales*	*Met Goal?*
5	Talos Bouras	250	486	415	1151	28775	
6	Leisa Malimali	74	88	101	263	6575	
7	Brian Simpson	389	303	422	1114	27850	
8	Amy Wyatt	346	381	502	1229	30725	Yes
9	**Monthly Total**	**1059**	**1258**	**1440**	**3757**		
10							
11	Average	264.75	314.5	360	939.25		
12	Maximum	389	486	502	1229		
13	Minimum	74	88	101	263		
14	Count	4	4	4	4		
15	Goal					30000	

This worksheet sums the monthly totals for all team members as well as the quarterly sales for each.

	A	B	C	D	E
1	**Sales Department**				
2	*Projected Net Profit*				
3		*Base*	*2%*	*5%*	*-5%*
4	Product Sales	$ 53,200	54,264	55,860	50,540
5	Contracts	241,000	245,820	253,050	228,950
6	**Total Revenue**	$ 294,200	$ 300,084	$ 308,910	$ 279,490
7					
8	Fixed Operating Cost	101,400	101,400	101,400	101,400
9	Marketing Expense	15,000	15,000	15,000	15,000
10	Commissions	27,824	28,380	29,215	26,433
11	**Total Costs**	$ 144,224	$ 144,780	$ 145,615	$ 142,833
12					
13	**Gross Profit**	$ 149,976	$ 155,304	$ 163,295	$ 136,657
14	**Net Profit**	$ 138,353	$ 143,267	$ 150,639	$ 126,066
15	**Gross Profit vs. Revenue**	51.0%	51.8%	52.9%	48.9%
16					
17	Contracts	482			
18	Average Contract	$ 500	Marketing	$ 15,000	
19	Product Commission Rate	7%	Fixed Cost	$ 101,400	
20	Contract Commission Rate	10%	Tax Rate	7.75%	

This worksheet reports the effect of various sales projections and costs on net profit.

Working with Formulas and Functions

Video Library   http://labyrinthelab.com/videos   Video Number: EX13-V0401

A formula is a math problem done in Excel. You can add, subtract, multiply, divide, and group cell contents to make your data work for you. A function is a prewritten formula that can simplify complex procedures for numbers and text. For instance, a function can be used to sum a group of numbers, to determine the payment amount on a loan, and to convert a number to text.

Using AutoSum to Create a SUM Formula

The AutoSum button automatically sums a column or row of numbers. When you click AutoSum, Excel starts the formula for you by entering =SUM() and proposes a range of adjacent cells within the parentheses. Excel first looks upward for a range to sum. If a range is not found there, it next looks left. You can accept the proposed range, which can be viewed in the Formula Bar, or drag in the worksheet to select a different range.

FROM THE RIBBON
Home→Editing
→AutoSum

FROM THE KEYBOARD
Alt + =

Excel 2013

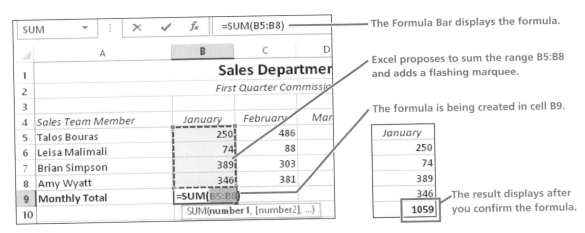

The Formula Bar displays the formula.

Excel proposes to sum the range B5:B8 and adds a flashing marquee.

The formula is being created in cell B9.

The result displays after you confirm the formula.

Average, Count, CountA, Max, and Min Functions

In addition to summing a group of numbers, the AutoSum button can perform a number of other calculations.

AutoSum and/or Status Bar Function	How Function Appears in Formula	Description
Sum	SUM	Adds the values in the cells
Average	AVERAGE	Averages the values in the cells
Count Numbers or Numerical Count	COUNT	Counts the number of values in the cells; cells containing text and blank cells are ignored
Count	COUNTA	Counts the number of nonblank cells
Max or Maximum	MAX	Returns the highest value in the cells
Min or Minimum	MIN	Returns the lowest value in the cells

TIP

Once you have entered a formula in a cell, you can use AutoFill to copy it to adjacent cells.

Status Bar Functions

The Status Bar, which is displayed at the bottom of the Excel window, can be customized to display a variety of functions including Average, Count, Numerical Count, Minimum, Maximum, and Sum. To customize the Status Bar, right-click anywhere on it and click to add or remove features. You can also customize additional features of the Status Bar, such as Zoom, Signatures, Overtype Mode, and Macro Recording.

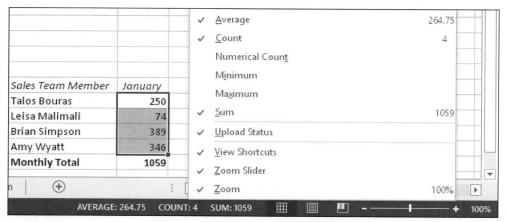

By default, Excel displays in the Status Bar the average, count of values, and sum of the selected range.

QUICK REFERENCE	USING AUTOSUM AND THE STATUS BAR FUNCTIONS
Task	**Procedure**
AutoSum a range of cells	■ Click in the desired cell and choose Home→Editing→AutoSum Σ. ■ Tap Enter to confirm the proposed range, or drag to select the correct range and tap Enter.
AutoSum across columns or down rows	■ Select the cell in the row directly below or column directly to the right of the data where you want the sums to appear and choose Home→Editing→AutoSum Σ.
Use Status Bar functions	■ Right-click the Status Bar and add or remove the desired functions. ■ Select the desired range, and view the results of the desired functions within the Status Bar.

DEVELOP YOUR SKILLS EX04-D01

Use AutoSum and Status Bar Functions

In this exercise, you will use AutoSum to calculate the monthly commission total for the sales team as well as the quarterly total for each sales team member.

1. Open **EX04-D01-Commissions** from the **Excel 2013 Lesson 04** folder, and save it as **`EX04-D01-Commissions-FirstInitialLastName`**.

   Replace the bracketed text with your first initial and last name. For example, if your name is Bethany Smith, your filename would look like this: EX04-D01-Commissions-BSmith. Notice the two tabs at the bottom of the window: Qtr 1 Commissions and Profit Projection.

2. With the **Qtr 1 Commissions** worksheet displayed, select **cell B9**.
3. Choose **Home→Editing→AutoSum** [Σ].

   Excel displays a marquee around the part of the spreadsheet where it thinks the formula should be applied. You can change this selection as necessary.

4. Follow these steps to complete the Sum formula:

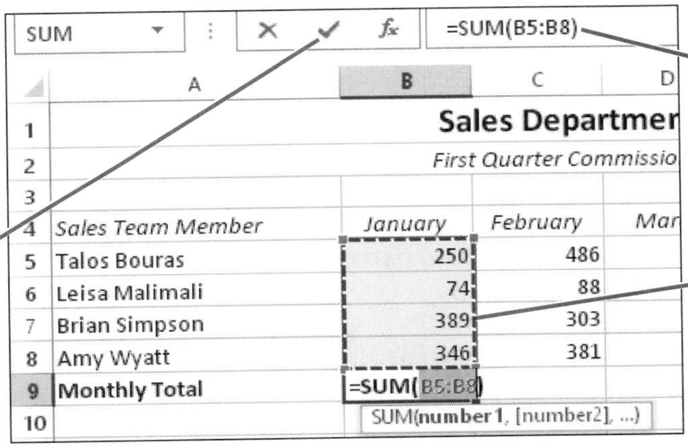

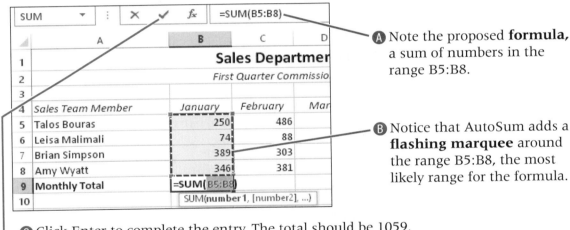

Ⓐ Note the proposed **formula,** a sum of numbers in the range B5:B8.

Ⓑ Notice that AutoSum adds a **flashing marquee** around the range B5:B8, the most likely range for the formula.

Ⓒ Click Enter to complete the entry. The total should be 1059.

5. Select **cell E7** and choose **Home→Editing→AutoSum** [Σ].

   Notice that, as there are no values above cell E7, Excel looked to the left to find a range to sum, B7:D7. Now, assume that you wanted only cells B7:C7 to be summed.

6. Follow these steps to override the proposed range:

Ⓐ Select the **range B7:C7**.

Ⓑ Notice that the new range, B7:C7, appears in the formula.

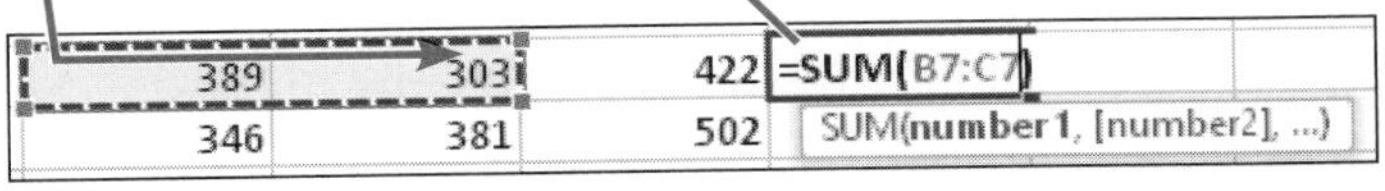

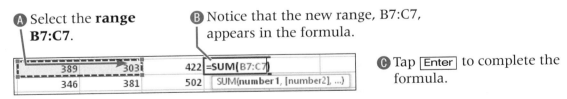

Ⓒ Tap [Enter] to complete the formula.

7. **Undo** [↶] the formula.

Use AutoFill to Extend a Formula

8. Follow these steps to AutoFill the formula in cell B9 into the cells to its right:

	A	B	C	D	E
1		**Sales Department**			
2		*First Quarter Commissions*			
3					
4	*Sales Team Member*	*January*	*February*	*March*	*Qtr 1 Total*
5	Talos Bouras	250	486	415	
6	Leisa Malimali	74	88	101	
7	Brian Simpson	389	303	422	
8	Amy Wyatt	346	381	502	
9	Monthly Total	1059			

Ⓒ Release the mouse button to fill the formula into the cells.

Ⓐ Select **cell B9**.

Ⓑ Position the mouse pointer over the **fill handle** at the bottom-right corner of the cell and drag to **cell E9**.

Cell E9 displays 0 because the cells above it are empty. You can create formulas that include empty cells and then enter data later.

9. Select the **range E5:E8**.

10. Choose **Home→Editing→AutoSum ∑** to calculate the quarterly totals.
    Excel created a formula in each cell of the selected range without requiring you to complete the formulas.

Qtr 1 Total
1151
263
1114
1229
3757

11. Delete the formulas in **range B9:E9** and **range E5:E8**.
    The data are returned to their original state.

12. Select the **range B5:E9** and click **AutoSum ∑**.
    The formula results appear in B9:E9 and E5:E8.

Explore Statistical Functions with AutoSum

13. Select **cell B11**.

14. Choose **Home→Editing→AutoSum ▼ menu button**.

15. Choose **Average** from the drop-down menu.
    Excel proposes the range B5:B10, which is incorrect.

16. Select the correct **range B5:B8** and tap Enter to complete the entry.
    The result should equal 264.75.

17. With **cell B12** selected, choose **Home→Editing→AutoSum ∑ ▾ menu button→Max**.

18. Select the correct **range B5:B8** and tap Enter to display the highest value in the range.
    The result should equal 389.

19. Select **cell B13** and choose **Home→Editing→AutoSum ▼ menu button→Min**.
    Min represents Minimum, or the lowest value.

20. Correct the range to **B5:B8** and then click **Enter** ☑ on the Formula Bar to display the lowest value in the range.

    The result should equal 74.

21. Select **cell B14** and choose **Home→Editing→AutoSum ▼ menu button**.

22. Choose **Count Numbers**, correct the range to **B5:B8**, and click **Enter** ☑.

23. Select **cell B6** and delete the contents.

    The formula recalculates the count as 3, and both the average and minimum formulas recalculate as well.

24. **Undo** ↺ the deletion.

Use Status Bar Functions

25. Select the **range B5:B8**.

26. Look at the Status Bar in the lower-right corner of the window to see that the sum value displayed equals the result in cell B9. **Save** the workbook and leave it open.

AVERAGE: 264.75   COUNT: 4   SUM: 1059

Excel 2013

Creating Formulas

Video Library   http://labyrinthelab.com/videos   Video Number: EX13-V0402

As you saw with AutoSum, functions begin with an equals (=) sign. Formulas begin with an equals sign as well, although Excel will automatically insert the equals sign if you first type a plus (+) or a minus (−) sign.

Cell and Range References

Formulas derive their power from the use of cell and range references. Using references in formulas ensures that formulas can be copied to other cells and that results are automatically recalculated when the data is changed in the referenced cell(s).

Do not type the results of calculations directly into cells. Always use formulas.

The Language of Excel Formulas

Formulas can include the standard arithmetic operators shown in the following table. Keep in mind that each formula you create will be entered into the same cell that displays the resulting calculation.

ARITHMETIC OPERATORS IN FORMULAS		
Operator	**Example**	**Comments**
+ (addition)	= B7+B11	Adds the values in B7 and B11
- (subtraction)	= B7–B11	Subtracts the value in B11 from the value in B7
* (multiplication)	= B7*B11	Multiplies the values in B7 and B11
/ (division)	= B7/B11	Divides the value in B7 by the value in B11
^ (exponentiation)	=B7^3	Raises the value in B7 to the third power (B7*B7*B7)
% (percent)	=B7*10%	Multiplies the value in B7 by 10% (0.10)
( ) (grouping)	=B7/(C4-C2)	Subtracts the value in C2 from the value in C4 and then divides B7 by the subtraction result

When typing a cell reference in a formula, you can type the column letter in lowercase and Excel will capitalize it for you.

"Please Excuse My Dear Aunt Sally"

Excel formulas follow the standard algebraic hierarchy. This means that the formula completes operations in the following order: parentheses, exponents, multiplication, division, addition, subtraction. The first letter of each of these is used in the mnemonic "Please Excuse My Dear Aunt Sally," which can be used to memorize this order.

To control the order of operations, you can use parentheses to cause Excel to add or subtract before multiplying or dividing. Review these examples to see how the order of operations works with and without parentheses.

$=53+7*5=53+35=88$ Multiplication and then addition

$=(53+7)*5=(60)*5=300$ Parentheses and then multiplication

Excel includes two additional items in the order of operations between parentheses and exponents. At the beginning of a formula, a minus (-) sign is interpreted as a negative. A percent sign is also considered as an operator.

Use the Keyboard to Create Formulas

In this exercise, you will use the keyboard to enter formulas into the spreadsheet.

1. Save your file as **EX04-D02-Commissions-FirstInitialLastName.**

2. Click the **Profit Projection** sheet
   tab at the bottom of the Excel
   window.

3. Select **cell B5** and view its formula in the Formula Bar.
   This formula multiplies the number of contracts (B17) by the average contract revenue (B18).

4. Select **cell B6** and use **AutoSum** to sum the sales in the **range B4:B5**.

5. In **cell B11**, sum the costs in the **range B8:B10**.
   The total costs result is not correct, but you will enter data in cells B9 and B10 in the next exercise.

6. Select **cell B13**, the Gross Profit for the Base column.

7. Type **=B6-B11** in the cell, and then tap [Enter] to complete the formula.
   In order to calculate the gross profit, you need to subtract the total costs (B11) from total revenue (B6).

8. Select **cell B15**, which is within the Gross Profit vs. Revenue row.

9. Type **=b13/b6** in the cell, tap [Enter], and **save** the workbook.
   In this worksheet, the cell has been formatted to display a percentage for you.

Using Cell References in Formulas

Video Library   http://labyrinthelab.com/videos   Video Number: EX13-V0403

A cell reference can be used to represent a cell or range of cells containing the values used in a formula. Cell references are one of three types: relative, absolute, or mixed.

Relative Cell References

A relative cell reference is one where the location is *relative* to the cell that contains the formula. For example, when you enter the formula =A3-B3 in cell C3, Excel notes that cell A3 is two cells to the left of the formula and that cell B3 is one cell to the left of the formula. When you copy the formula, the cell references update automatically. So, if the formula were copied to cell C4, the new formula would be =A4-B4. Excel updates the cell references so they are the same distance from cell C4 as were the cell references in the original formula in cell C3.

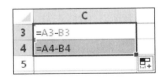

Excel 2013

Absolute Cell References

In some situations, you may not want references updated when a formula is moved or copied. You must use either absolute or mixed references in these situations. Absolute references within a formula always refer to the same cell, even when the formula is copied to another location. You create absolute references by placing dollar signs in front of the column and row components of the reference. For example, if the formula = $A$3-$B$3 were entered in cell C3, and then copied to cell C4, the formula within cell C4 would still read = $A$3-$B$3.

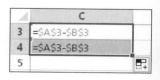

Mixed References

You can mix relative and absolute references. For example, the reference $C1 is a combination of an absolute reference to column C and a relative reference to row 1. This can be useful when copying a formula both across a row and down a column.

Using the F4 Function Key

The F4 function key can be used to insert the dollar signs within a cell reference. When F4 is first tapped, dollar signs are placed in front of the column and row components of the cell reference. A second tap of F4 places a dollar sign in front of only the row component, a third tap places one sign in front of only the column component, and a fourth tap removes all dollar signs.

The following table indicates what happens to different types of cell references when their formulas are copied to other locations.

Cell Reference	Type	Copy and Paste Action	Result When Pasted
B6	Relative	One column to the right	C6
B6	Relative	One row down	B7
$B$6	Absolute	One column to the right	$B$6
$B$6	Absolute	One row down	$B$6
$B6	Mixed	One column to the right	$B6
$B6	Mixed	One row down	$B7
B$6	Mixed	One column to the right	C$6
B$6	Mixed	One row down	B$6

Create Formulas Using Cell References

In this exercise, you will use absolute cell references to create formulas that can be copied to other cells.

1. Save your file as **EX04-D03-Commissions-FirstInitialLastName.**

2. Select **cell B9** and type **=** to begin a formula.

3. Select **cell D18** and tap F4.

If you have a keyboard that uses function keys for other purposes, you may have to tap F Lock to be able to utilize F4.

> *Notice $D$18 in the Formula Bar. In this case, you want the marketing expense to always reflect the value in cell D18.*

4. Tap Enter to complete the formula.

Calculate the Commissions Using Order of Operations

You will now enter a more complex formula to calculate the total commissions for product sales and contract sales.

5. Select **cell B10** and type **=** to begin a formula.

6. Select **cell B4** and type *****.
   Notice that when you click on cell B4, its cell reference is automatically placed within the formula. This is referred to as Point Mode, and it can help to minimize typing errors.

7. Select **cell B19** and tap F4.

8. Type **+** to continue the formula.

9. Select **cell B5** and type *****.

10. Select **cell B20** and tap F4.

11. Click **Enter** ☑.
    The result should be 27,824.

Calculate the Net Profit Using Parentheses

You will now create the formula =B13 * (1 - $D$20) to calculate the net profit.

12. Select **cell B14** and type **=**.

13. Select **cell B13** and type ***(1-** to continue the formula.

14. Select **cell D20** and tap F4.

15. Type **)** and tap Enter.
    The result should be $138,353.

Project a Sales Increase

*You will now create the formula =$B$4 * (1 + C$3) to project a 2 percent increase over the base product sales.*

16. Select **cell C4** and type an equals sign (=).

17. Select **cell B4** and tap $\boxed{F4}$.

18. Type ***(1+** to continue the formula.

19. Select **cell C3** and tap $\boxed{F4}$ two times to create the C$3 mixed cell reference.

20. Type **)** and tap $\boxed{\text{Enter}}$.
    The result should equal 54,264.

21. With **cell C5** selected, repeat **steps 16–20** (but using different cell references) to project a **2 percent increase** for base contract sales.
    The result should equal 245,820.

22. Save the workbook.

Modifying and Copying Formulas

Video Library   http://labyrinthelab.com/videos   Video Number: EX13-V0404

You can modify and copy formulas just like you edit and copy cells.

Modifying Formulas

You can edit a formula either in the Formula Bar or by double-clicking the formula cell. If you click or select a cell and enter a new formula, it replaces the previous contents.

When you select a formula to edit it, you will see colored lines around all cells referenced by the formula. This feature can help you track the formula elements.

Excel graphically displays the cells referenced by the formula, B13 and D20.

Circular References

A circular reference occurs when the formula refers to its own cell or to another formula that refers to that cell. For example, the formula in cell C6 is =B6*C6. Excel cannot complete the calculation because cell C6 is the formula cell, not a reference to a value. Excel displays an error message if you create a circular reference.

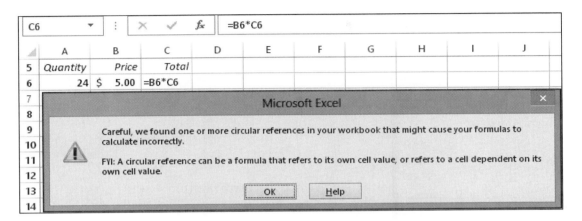

You must correct the formula manually after you close Help or the Circular Reference Warning message.

Copying Formulas

You can use either the Copy and Paste commands or AutoFill with formulas to copy them to new cells. If you use Auto Fill, the Auto Fill Options button will appear after you release the mouse button. Clicking this button allows you to customize your fill. The Fill Series option appears within the resulting list when you AutoFill values, but not when you AutoFill formulas.

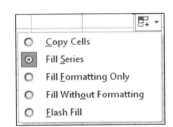

You can change what was copied in the cells through AutoFill with the Auto Fill Options button.

Modify and Copy Formulas

In this exercise, you will modify and copy formulas to complete your profit projection.

1. Save your file as **EX04-D04-Commissions-FirstInitialLastName.**

2. Select **cell B8**, and then follow these steps to edit the formula in the Formula Bar:

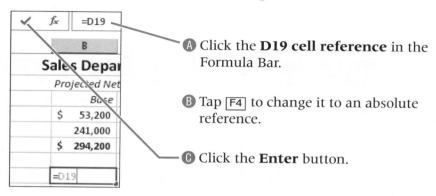

Ⓐ Click the **D19 cell reference** in the Formula Bar.

Ⓑ Tap F4 to change it to an absolute reference.

Ⓒ Click the **Enter** button.

3. Double-click **cell C6** to begin an in-cell edit.

4. Follow these steps to complete an in-cell edit:

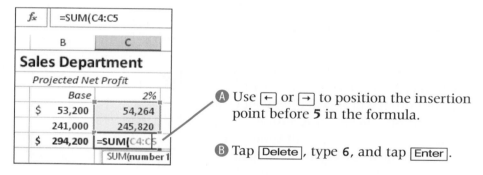

Ⓐ Use ← or → to position the insertion point before **5** in the formula.

Ⓑ Tap Delete, type **6**, and tap Enter.

Excel displays a Circular Reference Warning message because you referred to C6, the formula cell itself.

5. Choose **OK** in the Circular Reference Warning message.

6. **Undo** ⟲ the change.

Use Copy and Paste Commands to Copy a Formula

7. Select **cell B14** and then use Ctrl + C to **copy** the formula.

8. Select **cell C14** and then use Ctrl + V to **paste** the formula in the new cell.
   This method works great if you need to copy a formula to just one cell. You can use these commands to copy a formula to a range of cells as well.

9. Select the **range D14:E14** and then use Ctrl + V.
   The formula that you copied in step 6 is now pasted to the range of cells selected.

10. Tap Esc to cancel the marquee around cell B14.

11. Select **cell D14** and look at the formula in the Formula Bar.

    The relative cell reference now indicates cell D13, whereas the absolute cell reference is still looking to cell D20.

12. Follow these steps to use AutoFill to copy the formula:

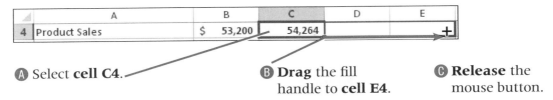

	A	B	C	D	E
4	Product Sales	$ 53,200	54,264		+

Ⓐ Select **cell C4**.　　Ⓑ **Drag** the fill handle to **cell E4**.　　Ⓒ **Release** the mouse button.

13. Use **AutoFill** to copy the formula from **cell C5** to the **range D5:E5**.

14. Select the **range B8:B15**.

15. Place your mouse pointer over the **fill handle** at the bottom right of the selected range.

16. When you see the thin cross **✛**, **drag right** until the highlight includes the cells in **column E** and then release the mouse.

	A	B	C	D	E
8	Fixed Operating Cost	101,400	101,400	101,400	101,400
9	Marketing Expense	15,000	15,000	15,000	15,000
10	Commissions	27,824	28,380	29,215	26,433
11	Total Costs	$ 144,224	$ 144,780	$ 145,615	$ 142,833
12					
13	Gross Profit	$ 149,976	$ 155,304	$ 163,295	$ 136,657
14	Net Profit	$ 138,353	$ 143,267	$ 150,639	$ 126,066
15	Gross Profit vs. Revenue	51.0%	51.8%	52.9%	48.9%
16					

17. Deselect the filled range, and **save** the workbook.

    Always deselect highlighted cells after performing an action to help avoid unintended changes.

Displaying and Printing Formulas

Video Library　http://labyrinthelab.com/videos　Video Number: EX13-V0405

Excel normally displays the results of formulas in worksheet cells, though you can choose to display the actual formulas. While formulas are displayed, Excel automatically widens columns to show more of the cell contents. Also, you can edit the formulas and print the worksheet with formulas displayed. When printing formulas, you may want to display the worksheet in Landscape orientation, due to the wider columns.

FROM THE RIBBON

Formulas→Formula Auditing→Show Formulas

FROM THE KEYBOARD

Ctrl + �}

Excel 2013

While formulas are shown, contents will be visible for those cells in which no formulas are used.

QUICK REFERENCE	VIEWING AND PRINTING FORMULAS
Task	**Procedure**
Display or hide formulas in a workbook	■ Choose Formulas→Formula Auditing→Show Formulas 📑.
Change page orientation	■ Choose Page Layout→Page Setup→Orientation→Landscape.
Print displayed formulas	■ Choose File→Print. ■ Choose any desired options in the Print tab and click Print.

DEVELOP YOUR SKILLS EX04-D05

Display Formulas in a Worksheet

In this exercise, you will display the formulas in the profit projection worksheet to see how it is constructed and to be able to troubleshoot any potentially inaccurate formulas.

1. Save your file as **EX04-D05-Commissions-FirstInitialLastName.**

2. Choose **Formulas**→**Formula Auditing**→**Show Formulas** 📑.

   You can use this feature to examine your formulas more closely.

3. Choose **Formulas**→**Formula Auditing**→**Show Formulas** 📑 again.

   The values are displayed once again.

Using Formula AutoComplete

Video Library   http://labyrinthelab.com/videos   Video Number: EX13-V0406

Formula AutoComplete assists you in creating and editing formulas. Once you type an equals (=) sign and any letter(s), Excel will display a list of functions beginning with the typed letter(s) below the active cell.

Functions Defined

A function is a predefined formula that performs calculations or returns a desired result. Most functions are constructed using similar basic rules, or syntax. This syntax also applies to the Min, Max, Average, Count, and CountA functions.

Begin formulas containing functions with an equals (=) sign.

Here, cells B6 and B8 are added to the range C10:C15.

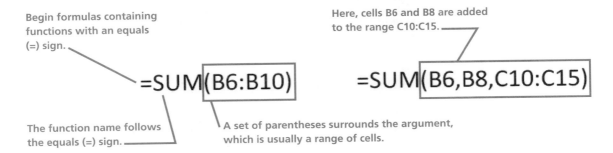

$$=SUM(B6:B10) \qquad =SUM(B6,B8,C10:C15)$$

The function name follows the equals (=) sign.

A set of parentheses surrounds the argument, which is usually a range of cells.

QUICK REFERENCE	USING FORMULA AUTOCOMPLETE TO ENTER A FORMULA INTO A CELL
Task	**Procedure**
Use Formula AutoComplete	■ Type an equals (=) sign and begin typing the formula.
	■ Double-click the formula in the list.
	■ Select the range where you will apply the formula.
	■ Type a closed parenthesis [)] to finish the formula.

DEVELOP YOUR SKILLS EX04-D06
Use Formula AutoComplete

In this exercise, you will use the Formula AutoComplete feature to create a formula.

1. Save your file as **EX04-D06-Commissions-FirstInitialLastName.**

2. Click the **Qtr 1 Commissions** worksheet tab.

3. Select **cell C11**.

4. Type **=ave** and observe the list that results.
   If you click on a function in the list, a ScreenTip will describe the function.

5. Double-click **AVERAGE**.

   Excel fills in the function name for you, but you must select the range.

=ave								
ƒₓ AVEDEV	Returns the average (arithmetic mean) of its arguments, which can be numbers or names, arrays, or references that							
ƒₓ AVERAGE	contain numbers							
ƒₓ AVERAGEA								
ƒₓ AVERAGEIF								
ƒₓ AVERAGEIFS								

6. Drag to select **cells C5:C8** as the formula range.

You do not include total rows or columns when completing most functions.

7. Tap Enter to complete the function.

   Excel added the parenthesis at the end of the formula for you. The result should be 314.5.

8. Select **cell C11**, use the fill handle to **copy** the function to the **range D11:E11**, and **save** the workbook.

   You now have the average commission for each month and the entire quarter.

Using Insert Function

Video Library http://labyrinthelab.com/videos Video Number: EX13-V0407

The Insert Function f_x button displays the Insert Function dialog box. It allows you to locate a function by typing a description or searching by category. When you locate the desired function and click OK, Excel displays the Function Arguments box, which helps you enter function arguments.

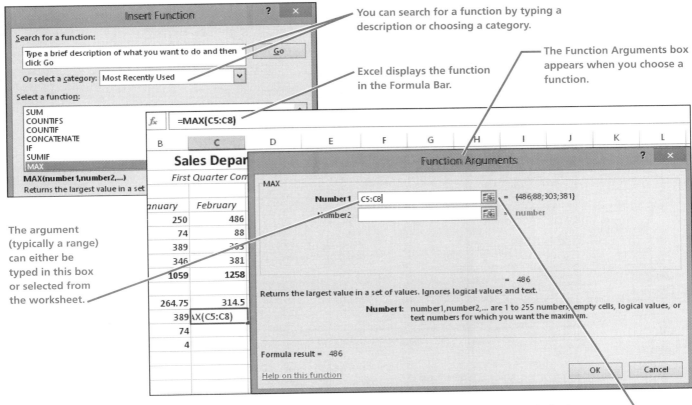

You can search for a function by typing a description or choosing a category.

Excel displays the function in the Formula Bar.

The Function Arguments box appears when you choose a function.

The argument (typically a range) can either be typed in this box or selected from the worksheet.

The Collapse button hides the Function Arguments box while you select the desired range.

Excel 2013

The Function Arguments dialog box can be moved by dragging its title bar to view the desired range on the worksheet.

QUICK REFERENCE	USING INSERT FUNCTION TO ENTER A FUNCTION IN A CELL
Task	**Procedure**
Create a function using Insert Function	■ Select the cell in which you wish to enter a function. ■ Click the Insert Function f_x button. ■ Choose the desired function; click OK. ■ Select the ranges to include in each function argument; click OK.

Use Insert Function

In this exercise, you will complete the Commissions worksheet by using the Insert Function command to create maximum and minimum functions.

1. Save your file as **EX04-D07-Commissions-FirstInitialLastName.**

2. Select **cell C12**.

3. Follow these steps to create the Maximum function:

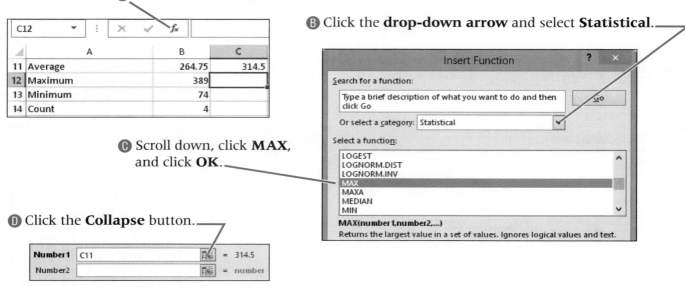

Ⓐ Click the **Insert Function** button.

Ⓑ Click the **drop-down arrow** and select **Statistical.**

Ⓒ Scroll down, click **MAX**, and click **OK**.

Ⓓ Click the **Collapse** button.

Ⓔ Select the **range C5:C8.**

Ⓕ Click the **Expand** button to redisplay the dialog box, and click **OK.**

4. Using the procedure from **step 3**, create the **Minimum** function in **cell C13**.

5. Create the **Count** function in **cell C14**.

6. Select the **range C12:C14**, copy the formulas to the **range D12:E14**, and save the workbook.

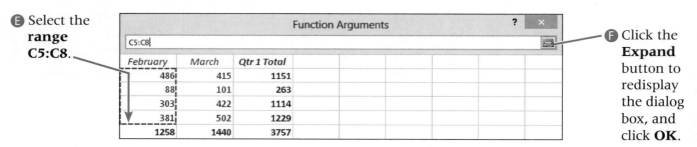

	A	B	C	D	E
11	Average	264.75	314.5	360	939.25
12	Maximum	389	486	502	1229
13	Minimum	74	88	101	263
14	Count	4	4	4	4

Creating Formulas with the IF Function

Video Library   http://labyrinthelab.com/videos   Video Number: EX13-V0408

Excel's IF function displays a value or text based on a logical test. It displays one of two results, depending on the outcome of your logical test. For example, if you offer customers a discount for purchases of $200 or more, an IF function could be used to display either the correct discount amount or $0. For purchases greater than $200, the IF function would calculate the discount; for purchases less than $200, the formula would insert $0.

IF Function Syntax

If you type the IF formula directly in its cell, you must add quotation (") marks around text arguments. If you use the Insert Function command, Excel adds the quotation marks for you.

The generic parts of the IF function are shown in the following table.

Function	Syntax
IF	IF(logical_test, value_if_true, value_if_false)

The following table outlines the arguments of the IF function.

Argument	Description
logical_test	The condition being checked using a comparison operator, such as =, >, <, >=, <=, or <> (not equal to)
value_if_true	The value, text in quotation (") marks, or calculation returned if the logical test result is found to be true
value_if_false	The value, text in quotation (") marks, or calculation returned if the logical test result is found to be false

How the IF Function Works

The formula =IF(C6>=200,C6*D6,0) is used as an example to explain the function result. Excel performs the logical test to determine whether the value in C6 is greater than or equal to 200. A value of 200 or more would evaluate as true. Any of the following would evaluate as false: a value less than 200, a blank cell, or text entered in cell C6. If the logical test proves true, the calculation C6*D6 is performed and the result displays in the formula cell. If the calculation proves false, the value 0 (zero) displays.

You may also use the IF function to display a text message or leave the cell blank. You may create complex calculations and even use other functions in arguments within an IF function, called nesting. Two examples that display text are shown in the following table.

Formula	Action if True	Action if False
IF(F3>150000, "Over Budget", "Within Budget")	The text *Over Budget* displays	The text *Within Budget* displays
IF(D6<=30, "", "Late")	The cell displays blank	The text *Late* displays

Excel 2013

If you type "" (quotation marks without a space between) as the value_if_true or value_if_false argument, Excel leaves the cell blank.

Use the IF Function

In this exercise, you will use the IF function to display a text message when a salesperson achieves at least $30,000 in quarterly sales.

1. Save your file as **EX04-D08-Commissions-FirstInitialLastName.**

2. Type the column heading **Sales** in **cell F4** and **Met Goal?** in **cell G4**.

3. Enter values in the **range F5:F8** as shown.

4. Type **Goal** in **cell A15** and **30000** in **cell F15**.

   You will create a formula that compares the value in the Sales cell with the goal of $30,000. If sales are equal or greater, the message Yes displays. Otherwise, the cell displays No.

	F	G
4	Sales	Met Goal?
5	28775	
6	6575	
7	27850	
8	30725	

5. Select **cell G5** and click the **Insert Function** 𝑓ₓ button in the Formula Bar.

6. Follow these steps to find the IF function:

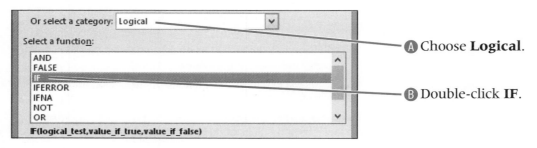

Ⓐ Choose **Logical**.

Ⓑ Double-click **IF**.

The Function Arguments dialog box appears for the IF function.

7. If necessary, move the Function Arguments dialog box out of the way by dragging its title bar until you can see **column G**.

8. Follow these steps to specify the IF function arguments:

Ⓐ Select **cell F5** in the worksheet, tap [Shift]+[>], and then tap [=] (for greater than or equal to).

Ⓑ Select **cell F15** (the $30,000 goal amount) and tap [F4].

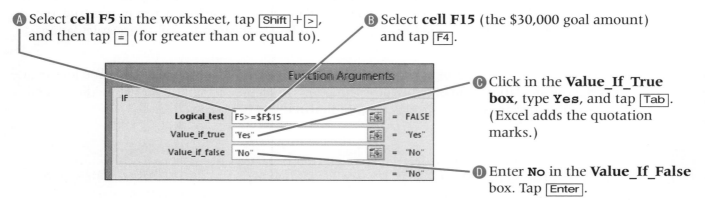

Ⓒ Click in the **Value_If_True box**, type **Yes**, and tap [Tab]. (Excel adds the quotation marks.)

Ⓓ Enter **No** in the **Value_If_False** box. Tap [Enter].

9. Review the completed formula in the Formula Bar.

The formula is =IF(F5>=$F$15,"Yes","No"). The message No appears in cell G5 because Talos Bouras' sales are not at least $30,000, the value in cell F15. The value_if_false argument applies.

10. Use **AutoFill** to copy the formula in **cell G5** down to the **range G6:G8**.

The cell for Amy Wyatt displays Yes as specified by your value_if_true argument. The cells for all other salespeople display No.

Edit the IF Function

11. Select **cell G5**.

12. In the Formula Bar, click between the quotation (") mark and the N, and tap Delete twice to delete *No*.

| *fx* | =IF(F5>=$F$15,"Yes","") |

13. Click **Enter** ✓ in the Formula Bar.

Cell G5 does not display a message because the value_if_false argument contains no text.

14. Use **AutoFill** to copy the formula in **cell G5** down to the **range G6:G8**, and **save** the workbook. Exit **Excel**.

Notice that the cells that previously displayed No in column G now display no message, as shown in the illustration below. The salespeople who met goal are easier to identify.

	A	B	C	D	E	F	G
4	Sales Team Member	January	February	March	Qtr 1 Total	Sales	Met Goal?
5	Talos Bouras	250	486	415	1151	28775	
6	Leisa Malimali	74	88	101	263	6575	
7	Brian Simpson	389	303	422	1114	27850	
8	Amy Wyatt	346	381	502	1229	30725	Yes
9	Monthly Total	1059	1258	1440	3757		
10							
11	Average	264.75	314.5	360	939.25		
12	Maximum	389	486	502	1229		
13	Minimum	74	88	101	263		
14	Count	4	4	4	4		
15	Goal					30000	

Concepts Review

To check your knowledge of the key concepts introduced in this lesson, complete the Concepts Review quiz by choosing the appropriate access option below.

If you are...	Then access the quiz by...
Using the Labyrinth Video Library	Going to http://labyrinthelab.com/videos
Using eLab	Logging in, choosing Content, and navigating to the Concepts Review quiz for this lesson
Not using the Labyrinth Video Library or eLab	Going to the student resource center for this book

Reinforce Your Skills

Create Simple Formulas

In this exercise, you will create and modify formulas using AutoSum, the keyboard, and Point Mode.

Work with Formulas and Functions

1. Start **Excel**. Open **EX04-R01-OrdersReturns** from the **Excel 2013 Lesson 04** folder and save it as **EX04-R01-OrdersReturns-[FirstInitialLastName]**.

2. Select **cell E4**.

3. Choose **Home→Editing→AutoSum Σ**, and confirm the formula.

4. Use **AutoFill** to copy the formula to **cells E5** and **E6**.
    Note that the Status Bar shows the sum of the range E4:E6.

Create Formulas

5. Select **cell B18**.

6. Type **=B4+B9+B14**, and tap Enter.

7. Use **AutoFill** to copy the formula to **cells C18** and **D18**.

Use Cell References in Formulas

8. Select **cell B19**.

9. Type **=** , select **cell B5**, and type **+**.

10. Select **cell B10** and type **+**.

11. Select **cell B15** and tap Enter.

12. Use **AutoFill** to copy the formula to **cells C19** and **D19**.
    The relative cell references update as you AutoFill the formula.

13. With the range **B19:D19** still highlighted, **AutoFill** to copy the formulas to **B20:D20**.
    Again, relative cell references allow you to AutoFill here and arrive at the correct formulas.

Modify and Copy Formulas

14. Highlight the range **E4:E6**.

15. Click **Copy** 📋.

16. Highlight the range **E9:E11**.

17. Click **Paste** from the Ribbon.

18. Highlight the range **E14:E16**.

19. Click **Paste**.

    Note that the marquee continued to surround E4:E6 after you pasted in step 17, so there was no need to click Copy prior to pasting in E14:E16.

20. Examine the formulas in the Formula Bar; then save and close the workbook. Exit **Excel**.

21. Submit your final file based on the guidelines provided by your instructor.

    To view examples of how your file or files should look at the end of this exercise, go to the student resource center.

REINFORCE YOUR SKILLS EX04-R02

Display Formulas and Use Functions

In this exercise, you will view formulas, use AutoComplete and Insert Function to create formulas, and use the IF Function.

Display and Print Formulas

1. Start **Excel**. Open **EX04-R02-Contracts** from the **Excel 2013 Lesson 04** folder and save it as **EX04-R02-Contracts-[FirstInitialLastName]**.

2. Tap ⌈Ctrl⌉+⌈`⌉ to display the worksheet formulas.

   The grave accent key ⌈`⌉ is above the ⌈Tab⌉ key.

3. Choose **View→Workbook Views→Page Layout View** 📄.

4. Take a few minutes to look at how the data and formulas display.

   Notice that Excel widened the columns so that most of the cell contents display. In this view, the worksheet fits on two pages.

5. Choose **Page Layout→Page Setup→Change Page Orientation→Landscape**.

   Landscape orientation prints across the wide edge of the paper, which can be useful for printing the formula view.

6. Choose **Page Layout→Page Setup→Change Page Orientation→Portrait**.

   Portrait orientation prints across the narrow edge of the paper, which is acceptable for printing this worksheet while formulas are hidden.

7. Click the **Normal View** button in the Status Bar at the bottom-right corner of the window.

8. Tap ⌈Ctrl⌉+⌈`⌉ to hide the formulas.

Use Formula AutoComplete

9. Select **cell A10** and edit the label to `Kids for Change Contracts - Prior Year`.

10. Select **cell B2** and use **AutoFill** to copy the series Qtr 2, Qtr 3, and Qtr 4 into the **range C2:E2**.

11. Select **cell B8**.

12. Begin typing the formula `=aver`, and then tap Tab to choose **AVERAGE** as the function.

13. Drag to select **B3:B6** and then tap Enter.
    The result should equal 33.

14. Use the **fill handle** to copy the formula across **row 8**.
    The average for each quarter of the current year is now displayed.

Use Insert Function

15. Select **cell B17**.

16. Click **Insert Function** from the Formula Bar.

17. Click the drop-down arrow and select **Statistical**.

18. Click the **Average** function from the list, and click **OK**.

19. Modify the range to **B12:B15** and confirm the formula.
    The result should equal 23.5.

20. Use the **fill handle** to copy the formula across **row 17**.

21. Select **cell B20**.

22. Use **point mode** to enter the formula =B7-B16, and complete the entry.
    The result should equal 38.

23. Use the **fill handle** to copy the formula across **row 20**.
    The number of contracts decreased for the third quarter from 76 to 72.

Create Formulas with the IF Function

24. Select **cell B21** and click **Insert Function** from the Formula Bar.

25. Select the **IF** function from the Logical category and click **OK**.
    The Function Arguments dialog box displays.

26. For the Logical Test entry, select **cell B20** in the worksheet, tap Shift + > for the greater-than symbol, and type **0**.

27. Tap Tab to complete the entry.

28. Type `Increase` in the Value If True box and tap Tab.

29. Type `Decrease` in the Value If False box and tap Enter.
    The result displays as Increase.

30. Use the **fill handle** to copy the formula across **row 21**; save and close the workbook. Exit **Excel**.

31. Submit your final files based on the guidelines provided by your instructor.
    To view examples of how your file or files should look at the end of this exercise, go to the student resource center.

Use Formulas to Complete a Worksheet

In this exercise, you will utilize multiple techniques to create appropriate formulas throughout a worksheet.

Work with Formulas and Functions

1. Start **Excel**. Open **EX04-R03-BenefitPlan** from the **Excel 2013 Lesson 04** folder and save it as **EX04-R03-BenefitPlan-[FirstInitialLastName]**.

2. Select **cell C12**, and choose **Home→Editing→AutoSum menu ▼→Min**.

3. Change the range within the formula to **C5:C9**.

4. Use the AutoSum menu to insert the **Maximum** for this range in **cell C13**.

Create Formulas

5. Select **cell J5**.

6. Type **=C5+E5+G5+I5** and tap ⏎Enter.

7. Use **AutoFill** to copy the formula to **J6:J10**.

Use Cell References in Formulas

8. Select **cell C10**.

9. Type **=sum(**, select the **range C5:C9**, and confirm the formula.

10. With **cell C10** selected, choose **Home→Clipboard→Copy**.

11. Select cell **E10**, hold down Ctrl, and select **cells G10 and I10**.
You can highlight nonadjacent cells by holding down the Ctrl *key.*

12. Choose **Home→Clipboard→Paste**.

13. Select **cell C15**.

14. Type **=** and select **cell C10**.

15. Type *****, select **cell J1**, and tap F4; confirm the formula.
Absolute formatting is needed for cell J1 so that the Match Percentage cell reference does not change when the formula is copied.

Modify and Copy Formulas

16. Highlight the **range C12:C13**.

17. Click **Copy** 📋.

18. Highlight the **range E12:E13**, hold down Ctrl, highlight **G12:G13** and **I12:I13**.

19. Click **Paste**.

20. Repeat the prior four steps to replicate the formula in **cell C15** to **cells E15, G15,** and **I15**.
Take a few minutes to examine the formulas in the Formula Bar.

Display and Print Formulas

21. Choose **Formulas→Formula Auditing→Show Formulas** 🔣.

22. Choose **View→Workbook Views→Page Layout View** 🖺.

    Take a few minutes to look at the way the data and formulas display.

    Notice that Excel widened the columns so that most of the cell contents display.

23. Choose **Page Layout→Page Setup→ Change Page Orientation→Landscape**.

    Landscape orientation prints across the wide edge of the paper, which is useful for printing the formula view.

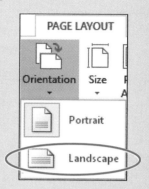

24. Click the **Normal View** button in the Status Bar.

25. Tap Ctrl + ` to hide the formulas.

Use Formulas AutoComplete

26. Select **cell C17**.

27. Begin typing the formula **=aver**, and tap Tab to choose **AVERAGE**.

28. Hold Ctrl to select **cells C15, E15, G15, and I15**, and then tap Enter.

Using Insert Function

29. Select **cell C14**.

30. Click **Insert Function** from the Formula Bar.

31. Click the drop-down arrow and select **Statistical**.

32. Click the **Count** function from the list, and click **OK**.

33. Modify the range to **C5:C9** and confirm the formula.

34. Copy the formula to cells **E14, G14, and I14**.

    Note that there were more contributions made in the second quarter than during any other quarter.

Create Formulas with the IF Function

35. Select **cell L5** and click **Insert Function** from the Formula Bar.

36. Select **IF** from the Logical category and click **OK**.

37. For the Logical Test entry, select **cell J5** in the worksheet, tap Shift + >, and select **cell K5**.

38. Tap Tab to complete the entry.

39. Type **Yes** in the Value If True box and tap Tab.

40. Type **No** in the Value If False box and tap Enter.

    The result displays as No because cells J5 and K5 contain equal values.

41. Use the **fill handle** to copy the formula down **column L**; save and close the workbook. Exit **Excel**.

42. Submit your final file based on the guidelines provided by your instructor.

Apply Your Skills

Create Formulas, and Use Absolute References

In the exercise, you will create a price sheet with formulas that use absolute references.

Work with Formulas and Functions

1. Start **Excel**. Open **EX04-A01-PriceChange** from the **Excel 2013 Lesson 04** folder and save it as **EX04-A01-PriceChange-[FirstInitialLastName]**.

2. Use **AutoSum** to add the original prices in **cell B13**.

Create Formulas

3. Sum the discounted prices for the **range C6:C11** in **cell C13**.
   This formula will yield results when the discounted prices are entered in the worksheet.

Use Cell References in Formulas

4. Calculate the discounted price in **cell C6** as `Original Price * (1 - Discount Rate)`. Use an **absolute reference** when referring to the discount rate in **cell B3**.

5. Copy the formula in **cell C6** down the column.
   Cell C6 was formatted for you so it displays the price with two decimal places.

6. Change the percentage in **cell B3** to **10%**, and watch the worksheet recalculate.

7. Change the percentage in **cell B3** back to **15%**, and watch the worksheet recalculate.
   You use cell references within formulas so that when changes are made, such as to the discount rate here, the formulas will recalculate properly.

Modify and Copy Formulas

8. Type **Cutlery Upgrade** in **cell A12**, and type **90** in **cell B12**.
   Notice that the discounted price in cell C12 has automatically displayed.

9. Ensure that the discounted price in cell C12 is calculated properly; save and close the workbook. Exit **Excel**.

10. Submit your final file based on the guidelines provided by your instructor.
    To view examples of how your file or files should look at the end of this exercise, go to the student resource center.

Use the AVERAGE and IF Functions

In this exercise, you will create an IF function to indicate whether a department met the safety goal each month. You will create formulas to total the safety incidents in a six-month period, and calculate the average number of incidents per month.

Display and Print Formulas

1. Start **Excel**. Open **EX04-A02-SafetyGoal** from the **Excel 2013 Lesson 04** folder and save it as **EX04-A02-SafetyGoal-[FirstInitialLastName]**.

2. Enter **January** in **cell A6**. **AutoFill** down **column A** to display the months January through June.

3. Display the worksheet formulas.

   Because you have not yet entered any formulas, nothing changes.

4. Hide the worksheet formulas.

   This ensures that you will see the results of any formulas entered in upcoming steps.

Use Formula AutoComplete

5. Use **AutoComplete** to enter the sum function in **cell B12**. Add all incidents in column B within this formula.

Use Insert Function

6. Use **Insert Function** to enter the **Average** function in **cell B14** to find the average number of safety incidents per month from January through June.

   Your formula should return an average of one incident per month.

Create Formulas with the IF Function

7. Use the **IF** function to create a formula in **cell C6** that indicates whether the department met its goal of no safety incidents during the month. Excel should display *Met Goal* if the incidents are equal to zero (0) and *Not Met* if the incidents are more than 0.

8. Copy the formula down the column for the months February through June; save and close the workbook. Exit **Excel**.

9. Submit your final file based on the guidelines provided by your instructor.

   To view examples of how your file or files should look at the end of this exercise, go to the student resource center.

Create a Financial Report

In this exercise, you will create a worksheet by entering data, creating formulas, and using absolute references. You will also save, print a section of, and close the workbook.

Work with Formulas and Functions

1. Start **Excel**. Open **EX04-A03-NetProfit** from the **Excel 2013 Lesson 04** folder and save it as **EX04-A03-NetProfit-[FirstInitialLastName]**.

2. Use **AutoSum** to add the revenue in **cell F4**.

Create Formulas

3. Type a formula in **cell B10** to sum the costs for Q1 in **column B**.
   Practice typing the cell references here. You will use Point Mode later.

4. **AutoFill** the quarter headings in **row 3** and the Total Costs formula in **row 10**.
   Ensure that you AutoFill the total costs through column F.

Use Cell References in Formulas

5. Use a formula to calculate employee costs in **cell B6**. The formula should multiply the revenue (**cell B4**) by the percentage (**cell B15**). Use a **mixed reference** to refer to the revenue and an **absolute reference** to refer to the cost percentage.

6. Copy the titles in the range **A6:A9** to the range **A15:A18**.

7. Use formulas to calculate the other costs in the range **B7:B9**. Each formula should multiply the revenue in **row 4** by the related cost percentage in **rows 16–18**.

8. Calculate the net profit in **cell B13** as `Gross Profit * (1 - Tax Rate)`. Once again, use an absolute reference when referring to the tax rate in **cell B19**.
   Your Net Profit should equal 169,740.

Modify and Copy Formulas

9. Modify the formula in **cell B12** to calculate Gross Profit as Revenue minus Total Costs.

10. Copy the range **B12:B13** to the range **C12:F13**.

11. Copy the formulas in the range **B6:B9** to the range **C6:E9**.

Display and Print Formulas

12. Display the worksheet formulas.
    Review the formulas to ensure that they have been entered correctly.

13. Hide the worksheet formulas.

Use Formula AutoComplete

14. Use **AutoComplete** to calculate Total Employee Costs in **cell F6**.

15. Copy the formula from **cell F6** to **cell F7**.

The Total Capital Expenditures in cell F7 should equal 377,300.

Use Insert Function

16. Use the **Insert Function Dialog Box** to sum the Total Materials Costs in **cell F8**.

17. Copy the formula from **cell F8** to **cell F9**.

Create Formulas with the IF Function

18. Create an IF Function in **cell H12** to determine if the Annual Gross Profit Goal in cell H4 has been met. Excel should display *Met Goal* if it has been met and *Missed Goal* if it has not been met. Save and close the workbook. Exit **Excel**.

Since the Gross Profit of 463,050 is less than the 500,000 goal in cell H4, Missed Goal *is displayed in cell H12.*

19. Submit your final file based on the guidelines provided by your instructor.

Extend Your Skills

In the course of working through the Extend Your Skills exercises, you will think critically as you use the skills taught in the lesson to complete the assigned projects. To evaluate your mastery and completion of the exercises, your instructor may use a rubric, with which more points are allotted according to performance characteristics. (The more you do, the more you earn!) Ask your instructor how your work will be evaluated.

EX04-E01 That's the Way I See It

You are known as the neighborhood Excel expert for small businesses! The chamber of commerce has asked you to create a worksheet analyzing three different retail businesses in your area so they can determine the profitability of the businesses in order to help develop marketing plans for the individual chamber members as well as the community at large. You will evaluate the local competition for each business, and create a formula that shows how well positioned the three companies are in the marketplace.

Open **EX04-E01-Competition** from the **Excel 2013 Lesson 04** folder and save it as **EX04-E01-Competition-[FirstInitialLastName]**.

Enter three companies and their industries at the top of the worksheet. Be sure to select companies from three different industries (electronics, women's clothing, etc.). Enter the direct competitors for each company within the spreadsheet, and create formulas that will display the number of competitors for each. Lastly, include a formula that designates companies with three or more competitors as having "High" competition, and companies with fewer than three competitors as having "Low" competition.

You will be evaluated based on the inclusion of all elements specified, your ability to follow directions, your ability to apply newly learned skills to a real-world situation, your creativity, and the relevance of your topic and/or data choice(s). Submit your final file based on the guidelines provided by your instructor.

EX04-E02 Be Your Own Boss

In this exercise, you will create a customer listing that shows the number of jobs performed for each customer of Blue Jean Landscaping, and the billings associated with each.

Open **EX04-E02-CustomerBase** from the **Excel 2013 Lesson 04** folder and save it as **EX04-E02-CustomerBase-[FirstInitialLastName]**.

Create formulas in the designated cells within column B to determine the total number of jobs for each company type and to count the number of companies of each type. For the Billings Increase columns, first place the increase percentages in a suitable location within the spreadsheet, and then use absolute formatting to create formulas for each company referencing these percentages. Format the worksheet using your knowledge of Excel, ensuring that all numbers are displayed properly. Since this is your company, write a paragraph with at least five sentences that summarizes the data you have calculated. Type the paragraph below the data. In it, explain what you have learned from the calculations and how you might change how you do business as a result.

You will be evaluated based on the inclusion of all elements specified, your ability to follow directions, your ability to apply newly learned skills to a real-world situation, your creativity, and your demonstration of an entrepreneurial spirit. Submit your final file based on the guidelines provided by your instructor.

Transfer Your Skills

In the course of working through the Transfer Your Skills exercises, you will use critical-thinking and creativity skills to complete the assigned projects using skills taught in the lesson. To evaluate your mastery and completion of the exercises, your instructor may use a rubric, with which more points are allotted according to performance characteristics. (The more you do, the more you earn!) Ask your instructor how your work will be evaluated.

EX04-T01 Use the Web as a Learning Tool

Throughout this book, you will be provided with an opportunity to use the Internet as a learning tool by completing WebQuests. According to the original creators of WebQuests, as described on their website (WebQuest.org), a WebQuest is "an inquiry-oriented activity in which most or all of the information used by learners is drawn from the web." To complete the WebQuest projects in this book, navigate to the student resource center and choose the WebQuest for the lesson on which you are currently working. The subject of each WebQuest will be relevant to the material found in the lesson.

WebQuest Subject: Utilizing the IF function when classifying restaurant chains as successful or unsuccessful

Submit your final file(s) based on the guidelines provided by your instructor.

EX04-T02 Demonstrate Proficiency

You have decided to recreate the Product Markup Worksheet for Stormy BBQ to make it more user-friendly. Specifically, you would like to remove the markup percentages from individual formulas. You want to replace them with a cell reference from the worksheet that contains the markup percentage.

Open **EX04-T02-ProductMarkup** from the **Excel 2013 Lesson 04** folder and save it as **EX04-T02-ProductMarkup-[FirstInitialLastName]**. Use the formula writing and absolute formatting skills that you have learned in this lesson to create the markup formulas described above and produce a more user-friendly worksheet. Format the worksheet as desired, ensuring that all numbers are properly formatted and will appear in a logical manner when printed.

Submit your final file based on the guidelines provided by your instructor.

Formatting Cell Contents, Basic Skills

LEARNING OBJECTIVES

After studying this lesson, you will be able to:

- Format worksheets using a variety of methods
- Control text to align and fit within cells
- Alter the appearance of numbers through a variety of methods
- Format cells with borders and fill colors
- Find and replace data and formatting

In this lesson, you will use Excel's formatting features to enhance your worksheets. You will also gain experience with Excel's Find and Replace commands, which allow you to quickly locate and change entries within worksheets. By the end of this lesson, you will have developed the skills necessary to create professional worksheets.

Formatting with Excel

green clean

The accountant for Green Clean, a janitorial product supplier and cleaning service contractor, has drafted an income statement, which you intend to use to examine quarterly revenue and expense figures. You will use many of Excel's formatting features to make the spreadsheet easier to read and understand. You will also create a workbook theme so uniform formatting may be applied to Green Clean's other worksheets.

	A	B	C	D	E
1	Green Clean				
2	Income Statement				
3	3rd Quarter [Current Year]				
4		July	August	September	Quarter Total
5	REVENUES				
6	Sales	254723	261378	188684	704785
7	Finance Charge Revenue	4702	3982	3370	12054
8	Total Revenues	259425	265360	192054	716839

	A	B	C	D	E
1	Green Clean				
2	Income Statement				
3	3rd Quarter [Current Year]				
4		July	August	September	Quarter Total
5	REVENUES				
6	Sales	$ 254,723	$ 261,378	$ 188,684	$ 704,785
7	Finance Charge Revenue	4,702	3,982	3,370	12,054
8	Total Revenues	$ 259,425	$ 265,360	$ 192,054	$ 716,839

The income statement is shown here before (top) and after (bottom) formatting changes have been made.

Formatting Worksheets

Video Library   http://labyrinthelab.com/videos   Video Number: EX13-V0501

Formatting deals with changing how the data in your worksheet looks, not with changing the data itself. In Excel and other Microsoft Office programs, you can format text by changing the font type, size, and color. You can also apply various font enhancements, including bold, italic, and underline. Excel's Live Preview feature allows you to preview many formatting changes by holding the mouse pointer over the option, so that you can see the formatting in action.

Formatting Entries

Formatting commands can be applied either through the Ribbon or by using the Mini toolbar. The Mini toolbar offers many of the same options as the Font group on the Home tab, but conveniently places them adjacent to the active cell. Different versions of the Mini toolbar will appear when you right-click a cell, and when you highlight a cell's contents.

FROM THE KEYBOARD
Ctrl+B for bold
Ctrl+I for italicize
Ctrl+U for underline

Formatting options can be selected from both the Ribbon and the Mini toolbar.

DEVELOP YOUR SKILLS EX05-D01

Format Cells with the Ribbon and Mini Toolbar

In this exercise, you will begin to format a worksheet by using both the Ribbon and the Mini toolbar.

1. Open **EX05-D01-IncomeStatement** file from the **EX2013 Lesson 05** folder and save it as
   `EX05-D01-IncomeStatement-[FirstInitialLastName]`.

   Replace the bracketed text with your first initial and last name. For example, if your name is Bethany Smith, your filename would look like this: EX05-D01-IncomeStatement-BSmith.

2. Follow these steps to change the font size of the entire worksheet:

Ⓐ Click the **Select All** button.

Ⓑ Choose **Home→Font→ Font Size menu ▼ button**.

Ⓒ Choose **12**.

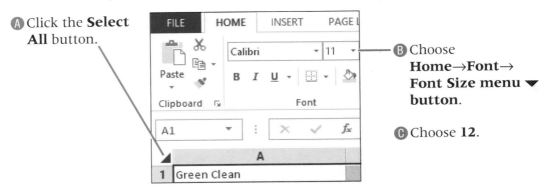

As you move the mouse pointer over the font size list, Excel shows how the worksheet would appear if each font size were selected.

Use the Mini Toolbar

3. Follow these steps to apply Bold formatting to cell A5:

Ⓐ Select **cell A5**. Ⓑ Double-click the word *REVENUES* in **cell A5** twice.

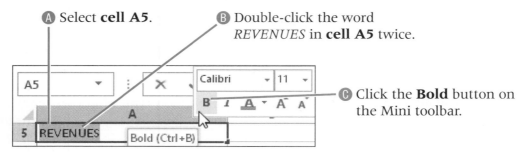

Ⓒ Click the **Bold** button on the Mini toolbar.

4. Right-click **cell A10** to display the Mini toolbar.

5. Click the **Bold** Ⓑ button on the Mini toolbar.

6. Save the file and leave it open; you will modify it throughout this lesson.

Using Excel's Alignment and Indent Features

Video Library   http://labyrinthelab.com/videos   Video Number: EX13-V0502

Excel allows you to alter how text is aligned within cells. In addition to the standard left, center, and right horizontal alignments, you can indent cells contents within a cell from either edge.

Aligning Entries

The Align Left, Center, and Align Right buttons let you align entries within cells. By default, text entries are left aligned and number entries are right aligned.

Indenting Cell Entries

The Increase Indent and Decrease Indent buttons let you offset entries from the edges of cells. If a cell entry is left aligned, it will indent from the left edge, and if it is right aligned, it will indent from the right edge.

FROM THE RIBBON

Home→Alignment →Align Left

Home→Alignment →Center

Home→Alignment →Align Right

FROM THE RIBBON

Home→Alignment →Increase Indent

Home→Alignment →Decrease Indent

Text is automatically left-aligned.

This entry is indented.

Numbers are automatically right-aligned.

Work with Alignment and Indent

In this exercise, you will set the alignment in cells as well as indent entries.

1. Save your file as **EX05-D02-IncomeStatement-[FirstInitialLastName]**.
2. Select the **range B4:E4**.
3. Choose **Home→Alignment→Align Right** 🔲.
4. Select the **range A6:A7**.
5. Choose **Home→Alignment→Increase Indent** 🔲.
6. Select the **range A11:A22**.
7. Choose **Home→Alignment→Increase Indent** 🔲.
8. Save the file and leave it open.

Excel 2013

Using Excel's Text Control Options

Video Library   http://labyrinthelab.com/videos   Video Number: EX13-V0503

The Alignment group on the Home tab provides options that allow you to merge cells and wrap lengthy text within a cell. Additionally, you can shrink text to fit within a cell.

Merging and Splitting Cells

The Merge Cells option allows you to combine cells. You can merge cells both vertically and horizontally, and merged cells behave as one large cell. The merged cell takes on the name of the top-left cell in the merged range. For example, if you merge cells A1:E1, the resulting merged cell will be named A1.

> **FROM THE RIBBON**
> Home→ Alignment→
> Merge & Center 🔲

The Merge & Center button merges selected cells and changes the alignment of the merged cell to center. This technique can be used to center a heading across columns, but it can only be used on one row at a time. You can split a merged and centered cell by clicking the Merge & Center button again.

	A	B	C	D	E
1			Green Clean		

Here, the original contents of cell A1 are merged and centered over the range A1:E1

If you merge two or more cells, each containing data, some of the data will be lost.

Merge Across

Unlike the Merge & Center, the Merge Across command is used to merge the contents of multiple rows simultaneously. For example, if you used Merge & Center on the range A1:D2, the result would be one large merged cell over this range. However, if you used Merge Across on this same range, the result would be two merged cells (neither of which is centered) within the ranges A1:D1 and A2:D2.

Wrapping Text

The Wrap Text option forces text to wrap within a cell, ensuring that no text will be cut off. The row height increases to accommodate the additional lines of wrapped text.

FROM THE RIBBON
Home→ Alignment
→Wrap Text

Entering a Line Break

To display text on a second line within a single cell, you can insert a line break.

FROM THE KEYBOARD
Alt + Enter to insert a line break

September	Quarter Total
188684	704785

The line break that forces "Total" to a second line can be removed by clicking here and tapping Delete.

Shrinking Text to Fit Within a Cell

There may be times when changing the width of a column or wrapping text is not appropriate, yet you still want all of the text within the cell to be displayed. The Shrink to Fit option allows you to reduce the text size of the cell entry to the exact size that fits the existing cell width.

QUICK REFERENCE	MERGING CELLS AND WRAPPING TEXT
Task	**Procedure**
Merge and center a range, one row	■ Select the desired cells and choose Home→Alignment→Merge & Center.
Merge and center a range, multiple adjacent rows	■ Select the desired cells. ■ Choose Home→Alignment→Merge & Center menu ▼→Merge Across. ■ Choose Home→Alignment→Center.
Unmerge cells	■ Select the desired cells and choose Home→Alignment→Merge & Center.
Wrap text within a cell	■ Select the desired cells and choose Home→Alignment→Wrap Text.
Shrink text to fit the column width	■ Right-click the desired cells and choose Format Cells. ■ On the Alignment tab, add a checkmark next to Shrink to Fit and click OK.

Control Text in Cells

In this exercise, you will merge and center cells as well as wrap text within a cell.

1. Save your file as **EX05-D03-IncomeStatement-[FirstInitialLastName]**.

2. Follow these steps to merge and center a range of cells:

Ⓐ Select the range **A1:E1**.   Ⓑ Choose **Home→Alignment→Merge & Center**.

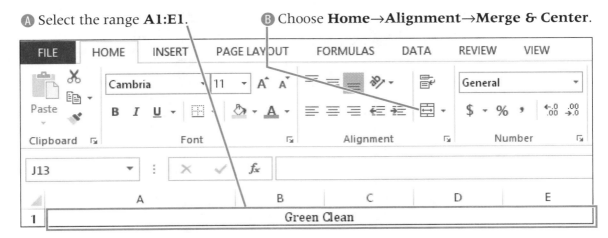

When you click in the merged cell, the Name Box displays A1 for the range.

Merge and Center on Multiple Adjacent Rows

3. Select the **range A2:E3**.

4. Choose **Home→Alignment→Merge & Center menu ▼→Merge Across**.

5. Choose **Home→Alignment→Center** 📄.
   This method is more efficient when merging multiple rows.

Wrap Text within a Cell

6. Select **cell A29**.

7. Choose **Home→Alignment→Wrap Text** 📄.
   The text will continue to wrap within the cell as it is edited and/or the column width is altered.

8. Follow these steps to manually enter a line break in a cell:

Ⓐ Select **cell E4**.   Ⓑ Click to the left of **Total** and tap [Backspace] to remove the space between words.

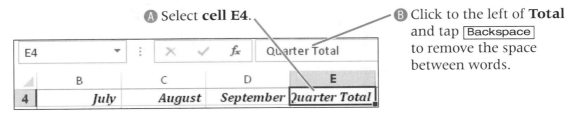

Ⓒ Hold down [Alt] and tap [Enter].

The line break will remain when text is edited and column widths are altered.

9. Tap [Enter] to complete the entry; save your file and leave it open.

Formatting Numbers

Video Library http://labyrinthelab.com/videos   Video Number: EX13-V0504

Number formats change the way numbers are displayed, although they do not change the actual numbers. Once a number format has been applied to a cell, it remains with the cell—even if the contents are deleted.

Number Format	Description
General	Numbers are formatted with the General format by default. This format does not apply any special formats to the numbers.
Comma Style	The Comma Style format inserts a comma after every third digit in the number. This format also inserts a decimal point and two decimal places, and indents the entry.
Currency	The Currency format is the same as the Comma Style format, except that it adds a dollar ($) sign in front of the number and does not indent the entry.
Accounting	The Accounting format is the same as Comma Style format, except that a dollar sign is placed at the left edge of the cell.
Percent Style	The Percent Style, also known as Percentage, inserts a percent (%) sign to the right of the number. The percentage is calculated by multiplying the number by 100.

If you begin an entry with a dollar sign, the Currency format will automatically be applied.

The following table provides several examples of formatted numbers.

Number Entered	Format	How the Number Is Displayed
5347.82	General	5347.82
5347.82	Comma with 0 decimal places	5,348
5347.82	Comma with 2 decimal places	5,347.82
5347.82	Currency with 0 decimal places	$5,348
5347.82	Currency with 2 decimal places	$5,347.82
.5347	Percentage with 0 decimal places	53%
.5347	Percentage with 2 decimal places	53.47%

Using the Number Command Group

The Number command group on the Home tab allows you to format numbers in many ways. If you click the dialog box launcher in the Number group, the Format Cells dialog box will appear, providing further formatting options.

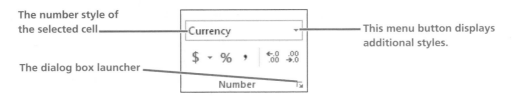

The number style of the selected cell

The dialog box launcher

This menu button displays additional styles.

Applying the Percent Style

The Percent Style, also called Percentage in Excel, adds a percent sign (%) after a number. To properly apply this style you must either apply the formatting before you type the number, or enter the value with two decimal places prior to applying the formatting.

How Numbers Display in Cells

Unlike text, numbers will not spill over into adjacent cells when they are too long. If the entry contains decimals, they will be rounded to as many decimal places as will fit within the cell. If the entry is formatted such that it cannot appear fully within the cell, number signs (###) will appear. In this instance you will widen the column to make the entry visible.

These formatted numbers are too wide to be visible.

	A	B	C	D	E
25	Net Income (Loss)	##########	##########	##########	##########
26					
27	Net Income to Total Revenues	0.271361665	0.311508894	-0.03845273	0.203218575

Decimals in these entries are rounded.

Adjusting Decimal Places

Most number formats display two decimal places by default. You can adjust the number of decimal places displayed by using the Increase Decimal and Decrease Decimal buttons. Decimals within your entry will automatically round as you add or remove decimal places.

FROM THE RIBBON

Home→Number→
Increase Decimal

Home→Number→
Decrease Decimal

Displaying Negative Numbers

Negative number displays can be either preceded by a minus sign or surrounded by parentheses. You can also display negative numbers in red. The Currency and Number options in the Format Cells dialog box allow you to choose the format for negative numbers.

This negative entry is displayed with a negative sign.

	A	B	C	D	E
25	Net Income (Loss)	70398	82662	-7385	145675
26					
27	Net Income to Total Revenues	0.271361665	0.311508894	(0.03845273)	0.203218575

This negative entry is displayed in red with parentheses.

Format Numbers

In this exercise, you will apply various number formatting options to the worksheet.

1. Save your file as **EX05-D04-IncomeStatement-[FirstInitialLastName]**.

2. Follow these steps to apply the Accounting format to a range of cells:

Ⓐ Select the **range B6:E6**.   Ⓑ Choose **Home→Number→ Accounting Number Format**.

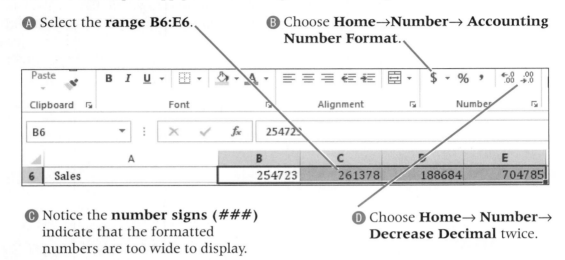

Ⓒ Notice the **number signs (###)** indicate that the formatted numbers are too wide to display.   Ⓓ Choose **Home→ Number→ Decrease Decimal** twice.

"Custom" is displayed as the number format on the Ribbon because you changed the number of decimal places of the Accounting format.

3. Select the **range B7:E7**.

4. Choose **Home→Number→Comma Style** ▾.

5. Choose **Home→ Number→Decrease Decimal** twice.

6. Select the **range B8:E8**, hold down Ctrl, and select the **range B11:E11**.

Remember that by using Ctrl, you can select multiple ranges to which you can apply formatting.

7. Choose **Home→Number→Accounting Number Format** $.

8. Choose **Home→Number→Decrease Decimal** twice.

9. Repeat **steps 7–8** to apply **Accounting Number Format** with no decimals to the **ranges B23:E23** and **B25:E25**.

Alternatively, after highlighting these two ranges, tapping the F4 key would have replicated the formatting applied above. Using the F4 key to repeat the most recent command (or most recent set of formatting changes) can save a significant amount of time.

Use Comma Style

10. Select the **range B12:E22**.

11. Apply **Comma Style** formatting with no decimals to the selection.

Notice that the 0 entry in cell C16 now displays as a hyphen (–) because Comma Style formatting has been applied.

12. Follow these steps to apply the Percent Style to a range of cells:

Ⓐ Select the **range B27:E27**.　　Ⓑ Choose **Home→Number→ Percent Style**.

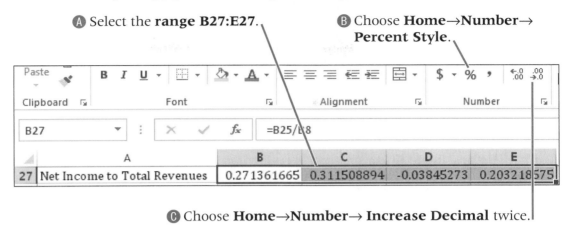

Ⓒ Choose **Home→Number→ Increase Decimal** twice.

13. Save your file and leave it open.

Using the Format Cells Dialog Box

Video Library　http://labyrinthelab.com/videos　Video Number: EX13-V0505

The Format Cells dialog box contains six tabs that allow you to format your worksheet. Some options in this dialog box are not available on the Ribbon; you must use these tabs to access them.

These dialog box launchers allow you to access the Format Cells dialog box.

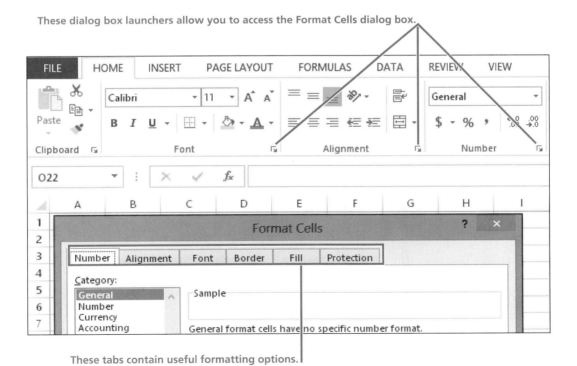

These tabs contain useful formatting options.

Applying Borders and Fills to Cells

Borders are lines around the cell edges that both print and display in the worksheet. Fills are background shading and pattern effects that fill entire cells. Keep in mind that "less is more" when applying colors and other formatting.

Applying Borders

The Borders button lets you add borders to cell edges. When you click the Borders menu ▼ button, a list of options appears.

FROM THE RIBBON

Home→Font→
Borders

The Borders menu ▼ button displays the image of the last border applied.

Aside from the All Borders option, each border must be applied one edge at a time to all cells in a selected range.

Applying Fill Colors and Patterns

The Fill Color button lets you fill the background of selected cells with color. When you click the Fill Color menu button, a palette of colors appears. You can apply a color to all selected cells by choosing it from the palette, and can remove a color by selecting the No Fill option.

FROM THE RIBBON

Home→Font→
Fill Color

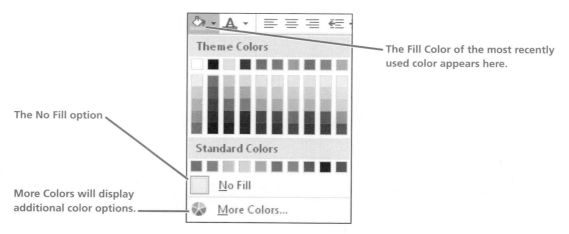

The No Fill option

More Colors will display additional color options.

The Fill Color of the most recently used color appears here.

Printing a test version of a worksheet allows you to see how your color choices will print. This is especially important for grayscale printers.

Format with the Format Cells Dialog Box

In this exercise, you will apply borders and fill colors to the worksheet.

1. Save your file as **EX05-D05-IncomeStatement-[FirstInitialLastName]**.

2. Select the **range A1:E27**.

3. Choose **Home→Font→Borders menu ▼→More Borders**.

4. Follow these steps to apply the border formatting:

Ⓐ Click this line style.   Ⓑ Click the **Outline** option.

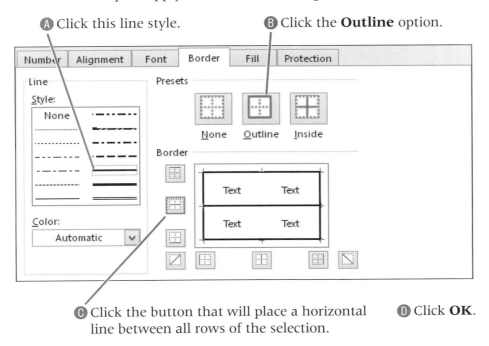

Ⓒ Click the button that will place a horizontal   Ⓓ Click **OK**.
line between all rows of the selection.

The Borders button now displays this icon ⊞, which represents the More Borders option—the last option chosen from the Ribbon.

5. Use ⌈Ctrl⌉ + ⌈Z⌉ to undo the borders.

6. Select the **range B7:E7**, hold down ⌈Ctrl⌉, and select the **range B22:E22**. Release ⌈Ctrl⌉.

7. Click the **Borders menu ▼** button.

8. Choose **Bottom Border** to place a border along the bottom of the selected cells.
A border will appear along the bottom of both of the selected ranges.

9. Select the **range B25:E25**.

10. Click the **Borders menu ▼ button** and choose **Top and Double Bottom Border**.

Excel 2013

Apply Fill Color to a Range

11. Select the **range A5:E5**, hold down Ctrl, and select the **range A10:E10**. Release Ctrl.

12. Follow these steps to apply a fill color to the selected ranges:

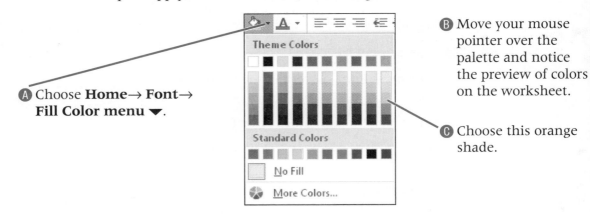

(A) Choose **Home→ Font→ Fill Color menu** ▼.

(B) Move your mouse pointer over the palette and notice the preview of colors on the worksheet.

(C) Choose this orange shade.

13. Click away from the selection to view the color in the selected ranges. Save your file and leave it open.

Using Excel's Find and Replace Commands

Video Library http://labyrinthelab.com/videos Video Number: EX13-V0506

Excel's Find command can perform searches for a particular word, number, cell reference, formula, or format within a worksheet or an entire workbook. The Replace feature helps you to find an item and replace it with a specified item. While using these features you should keep in mind that Excel searches for text without regard for upper- or lowercase, but will replace text only with the exact case you type.

FROM THE KEYBOARD
Ctrl+F to find
Ctrl+H to replace

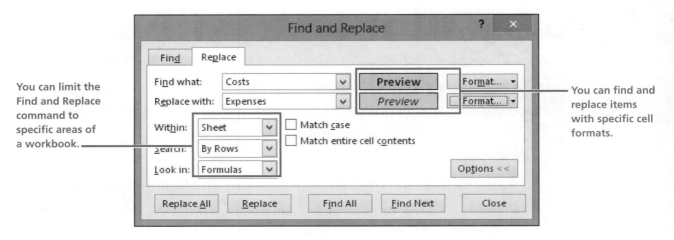

You can limit the Find and Replace command to specific areas of a workbook.

You can find and replace items with specific cell formats.

QUICK REFERENCE	FINDING AND REPLACING DATA AND FORMATS
Task	**Procedure**
Find text or formatting	■ Choose Home→Editing→Find & Select→Find.
	■ Indicate your search parameters and click Find Next or Find All.
Find and replace text or formatting	■ Choose Home→Editing→Find & Select→Replace.
	■ Indicate your search parameters and desired replacements.
	■ Click Replace (All) or Find (All), as appropriate.
Clear all find and replace options	■ Choose Home→Editing→Find & Select→Replace, clear all typed entries, and click Options.
	■ Select the top Format menu ▼ button and choose Clear Find Format.
	■ Select the bottom Format menu ▼ button and choose Clear Replace Format.

DEVELOP YOUR SKILLS EX05-D06

Find and Replace Entries

In this exercise, you will find and replace text as well as formatting.

1. Save your file as **EX05-D06-IncomeStatement-[FirstInitialLastName]**.

2. Choose **Home→Editing→Find & Select 🔍→Replace**.

   The Find and Replace dialog box opens.

3. Follow these steps to prepare to replace all instances of *Costs* with *Expenses*.

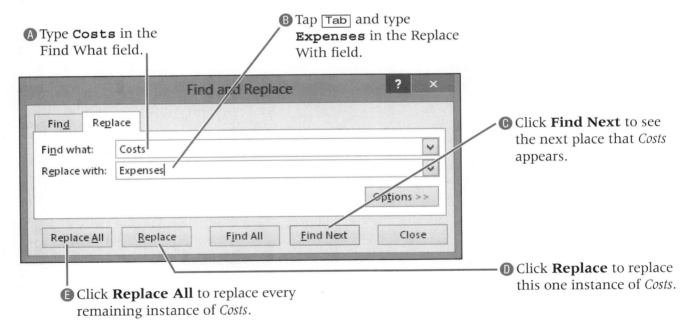

Ⓐ Type **Costs** in the Find What field.

Ⓑ Tap Tab and type **Expenses** in the Replace With field.

Ⓒ Click **Find Next** to see the next place that *Costs* appears.

Ⓓ Click **Replace** to replace this one instance of *Costs*.

Ⓔ Click **Replace All** to replace every remaining instance of *Costs*.

4. Click **OK** to acknowledge the total number of replacements.

   Leave the Find and Replace dialog box open.

Find and Replace Formatting

5. Click the **Options** button in the Find and Replace dialog box.

6. Follow these steps to begin setting the formatting to be found:

Ⓐ Delete the contents of the **Find What** and **Replace With** boxes.

Ⓑ Click the top **Format menu** ▼ **button** and select **Choose Format From Cell.**

Ⓒ Select **cell B4.**

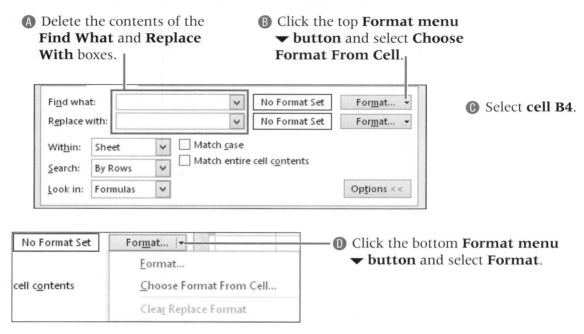

Ⓓ Click the bottom **Format menu** ▼ **button** and select **Format**.

7. Follow these steps to continue defining the format:

Ⓐ Select the **Font** tab.

Ⓑ Choose **Bold** and **11** for the font style and size.

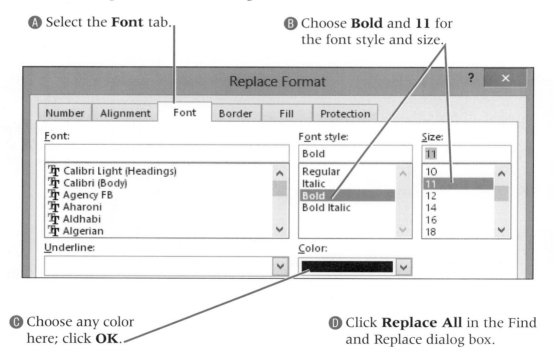

Ⓒ Choose any color here; click **OK**.

Ⓓ Click **Replace All** in the Find and Replace dialog box.

8. Click **OK** in the dialog box that appears.

   All instances of formatting that are the same as that in cell B4 are replaced with the new formatting you chose. Because the formatting in cell E4 is not identical to B4, cell E4 does not change.

Clear Find and Replace Criteria

The Find and Replace criteria remain set even after the dialog box is closed. You must clear the criteria before performing another Find or Replace operation. (Exiting Excel also clears the dialog box.)

9. Click the top **Format menu ▼ button** and choose **Clear Find Format**.

10. Click the bottom **Format menu ▼ button** and choose **Clear Replace Format**.

11. Click **Close** to exit the Find and Replace dialog box.

12. Select **cell E4**.

13. Choose **Home→Font→Font Color menu ▼ button** and choose the same fill color applied to the **range B4:D4**.

    All entries within row 4 now appear uniform.

14. Save and then close your file. Exit **Excel**.

Concepts Review

To check your knowledge of the key concepts introduced in this lesson, complete the Concepts Review quiz by choosing the appropriate access option below.

If you are...	Then access the quiz by...
Using the Labyrinth Video Library	Going to http://labyrinthelab.com/videos
Using eLab	Logging in, choosing Content, and navigating to the Concepts Review quiz for this lesson
Not using the Labyrinth Video Library or eLab	Going to the student resource center for this book

Reinforce Your Skills

Format a Worksheet

In this exercise, you will format a worksheet using commands available on the Ribbon and on the Mini toolbar.

Format Worksheets

1. Start **Excel**. Open **EX05-R01-Budget** from the **EX2013 Lesson 05** folder and save it as **EX05-R01-Budget-[FirstInitialLastName]**.

2. Change the font for the entire worksheet to **Calibri**.
   Only those entries originally displayed in a font other than Calibri will change.

3. Select **cells A1, A7, and A15** using the ⌨Ctrl⌨ key.

4. Choose **Home→Font→Bold** B.

5. Right-click **cell A25** and choose **Bold** B from the Mini toolbar.

Use Excel's Alignment and Indent Features

6. Select the **range A8:A12**.

7. Choose **Home→Alignment→Increase Indent** ⌨.
   This indentation distinguishes the revenue items from the header and total rows.

8. Select the **range A16:A23**.

9. Choose **Home→Alignment→Increase Indent** ⌨.

10. Select **cell A4**.

11. Choose **Home→Alignment→Align Right** ⌨.

Use Excel's Text Control Options

12. Select the **range A1:C2**.

13. Choose **Home→Alignment→Merge & Center menu ▾→Merge Across**.
    The Merge Across command allows you to merge multiple rows at once.

14. Double-click **cell B6** to begin in-cell editing.

15. Move the insertion point just to the left of the *A* in *Actual*, and tap ⌨Backspace⌨ to remove the space between words.

16. Press ⌨Alt⌨ + ⌨Enter⌨ to insert a line break, and tap ⌨Enter⌨ to confirm the entry.

17. Repeat **steps 15–16** to insert a line break in the text of **cell C6**.

18. Align the text in the **range B6:C6** with the numbers in the columns.

Format Numbers

19. Select the **ranges B8:C8**, **B13:C13**, and **B16:C16** using Ctrl.

20. Choose **Home→Number→Accounting Number Format $**.
    Leave the default two decimal places as is.

21. Select the **range B24:C25**.

22. Right-click a selected cell and choose **Accounting Number Format $** from the Mini toolbar.

23. Select the **range B9:C12**.

24. Using the method of your choice, apply **Comma Style** with two decimal places to the selection.
    This ensures that no dollar sign is displayed for those amounts that are not located on the top or bottom row within the revenue section.

25. Select the **range B17:C23**.

26. Press Ctrl + Y to repeat the most recent action.
    Comma Style is applied to the selection.

27. Select **cell C4**.

28. Choose **Home→Number→Number Format menu ▼ button** and choose **Currency**.
    Notice that the dollar sign ($) displays next to the number. Compare this to the dollar sign placement in cell C8, to which you applied Accounting Number Format.

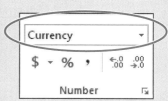

29. Save and then close the file; exit from **Excel**.

30. Submit your file based on guidelines provided by your instructor.
    To view examples of how your file or files should look at the end of this exercise, go to the student resource center.

REINFORCE YOUR SKILLS EX05-R02
Design a Budget Worksheet

In this exercise, you will format a budget worksheet using the Format Cells dialog box and the Ribbon.

Use the Format Cells Dialog Box

1. Start **Excel**. Open **EX05-R02-WebsiteBudget** from the **EX2013 Lesson 05** folder and save it as **EX05-R02-WebsiteBudget-[FirstInitialLastName]**.

2. Select **cell A6**.

3. Choose **Home→Font→dialog box launcher** to display the Format Cells dialog box.
   The Format Cells dialog box can be used to easily apply a wide variety of formatting.

4. Select the **Bold** font style and click **OK**.

Apply Borders and Fills to Cells

5. Select **cell A1**.

   Notice that the Merged Cell A1:B1 is highlighted.

6. Choose **Home→Font→Fill Color menu** ▼ button and select **Olive Green, Accent 3, Lighter 40%.**

7. Select the **range A3:B3**.

8. Choose **Home→Font→Borders menu** ▼**→Top and Bottom Border**.

   Borders offer another formatting option that can distinguish cells within a worksheet.

Use Excel's Find and Replace Command

9. Click **cell A1** and choose **Home→Editing→Find & Select→Replace**.

10. Enter **spending plan** in the **Find What** box and **Budget** in the **Replace With** box.

    You do not have to use a capital "S" or "P" in the Find What box. If you want the replacement text to be capitalized though, you must type it that way in the Replace With box.

11. Click **Replace All**, click **OK** in the dialog box that appears, and click **Close**.

12. Save and then close the file; exit from **Excel**.

13. Submit your final file based on the guidelines provided by your instructor.

    To view examples of how your file or files should look at the end of this exercise, go to the student resource center.

REINFORCE YOUR SKILLS EX05-R03
Format a Balance Sheet

In this exercise, you will format a balance sheet using a variety of commands and techniques.

Format Worksheets

1. Start **Excel**. Open **EX05-R03-BalanceSheet** from the **EX2013 Lesson 05** folder and save it as **EX05-R03-BalanceSheet-[FirstInitialLastName]**.

2. Change the font for the entire worksheet to **Calibri**.

   Regardless of which font you apply, in order to maintain consistency it should be applied throughout the entire worksheet.

3. Select **cells A5, A12, and A17** using the Ctrl key.

4. Choose **Home→Font→Bold** B.

   These headings should be distinguished from the rest of the worksheet in some manner, and although you used bold here, other formatting options would also have been effective.

5. Right-click **cell B4** and choose **Bold** B from the Mini toolbar.

Use Excel's Alignment and Indent Features

6. Select the **range A6:A9**.

7. Choose **Home→Alignment→Increase Indent** 📑.

8. Select the **range A13:A14,** and **cell A18** using ⌈Ctrl⌉.

9. Choose **Home→Alignment→Increase Indent** 📑.

10. Select **cell B4**.

11. Choose **Home→Alignment→Center** 📄.

Use Excel's Text Control Options

12. Select the **range A1:B1**.

13. Choose **Home→Alignment→Merge & Center** 📄.

14. Select the **range A2:B3**.

15. Choose **Home→Alignment→Merge & Center menu** ▼→**Merge Across**.

The Merge Across command allows you to merge multiple rows at once, but does not center the cell contents.

16. With the **range A2:B3** still selected, choose **Home→Alignment→Center**.

17. Double-click **cell A19** to begin in-cell editing.

18. Move the insertion point just to the left of the *O* in *Owners'* and tap ⌈Backspace⌉ to remove the space between words.

19. Use ⌈Alt⌉+⌈Enter⌉ to insert a line break.

You can reduce column widths throughout a worksheet by using this technique to force text to wrap where you choose within a cell.

20. Right-click **cell A13**.

21. Choose **Format Cells**, insert a checkmark beside **Shrink to Fit** under the Alignment tab, and click **OK**.

Format Numbers

22. Select **cells B6, B10, and B13** using ⌈Ctrl⌉.

23. Choose **Home→Number→Accounting Number Format** ⌈$⌉.

Leave the default two decimal places as is.

24. Select the **range B18:B19** and **cell B15** using ⌈Ctrl⌉.

25. Right-click a selected cell and choose **Accounting Number Format** ⌈$⌉ from the Mini toolbar.

26. Select the **range B7:B9** and **cell B14** using ⌈Ctrl⌉.

27. Using the method of your choice, apply **Comma Style** with two decimal places.

Use the Format Cells Dialog Box

28. Select the **range A1:A3**.

29. Choose **Home→Font→dialog box launcher** to display the Format Cells dialog box.

The Format Cells dialog box can be used to easily apply a wide variety of formatting.

30. Select the **Bold** font style and click **OK**.

Apply Borders and Fills to Cells

31. Ensure that the **range A1:A3** is still selected.

Notice that the Merged Cells within the first three rows are highlighted.

32. Choose **Home→Font→Fill Color menu** ▼ button and select **Standard Light Green**.

This fill color results in the selected cells standing out from the surrounding data.

33. Select **cells B10 and B19** using Ctrl.

34. Choose **Home→Font→Borders menu** ▼→**Top and Double Bottom Border**.

Use Excel's Find and Replace Command

35. Click **cell A1** then choose **Home→Editing→Find & Select→Replace**.

36. Enter `resources` in the **Find What** box and `Assets` in the **Replace With** box.

You do not have to use a capital "R" in the Find What box. If you want the replacement text to be capitalized though, you must type it that way in the Replace With box.

37. Click **Replace All**, click **OK** in the dialog box that appears, and click **Close**.

38. Save and then close the file; exit from **Excel**.

39. Submit your final file based on the guidelines provided by your instructor.

Apply Your Skills

Format Text and Numbers

In this exercise, you will format text and numbers.

Format Worksheets and Use Excel's Alignment and Indent Features

1. Start **Excel**. Open **EX05-A01-Inventory** from the **EX2013 Lesson 05** folder and save it as **EX05-A01-Inventory-[FirstInitialLastName]**.

2. Apply **bold** formatting to the entries in **rows 4 and 12**.
   Bold formatting makes these column headers stand out from the other worksheet entries.

3. Format the title in **cell A1** with **bold,** and change the font size to **14**.

4. Right-align the entries in the **ranges D4:E4** and **D12:E12**.
   These headers are now aligned with the numbers listed below.

5. Indent the entries in the **ranges A5:A9** and **A13:A16**.

Use Excel's Text Control Options and Format Numbers

6. Merge and center the titles in **cells A1 and A2** across **columns A–E**.

7. Change **cell D4** to `Retail Price` and insert a **line break** so each word is on a separate line.

8. Insert a **line break** in **cell D12** so each word is on a separate line.

9. Format **cells D5 and D13** in **Currency Style** with two decimals.

10. Format the **ranges D6:D9** and **D14:D16** in **Number** style.

11. Format the **ranges E5:E10** and **E13:E17** in **Comma Style** with zero decimals.

12. Save and then close the file; exit from **Excel**.

13. Submit your final file based on the guidelines provided by your instructor.
    To view examples of how your file or files should look at the end of this exercise, go to the student resource center.

Add Borders and Fill Color, and Use Find and Replace

In this exercise, you will finalize the appearance of a worksheet by applying borders and fill colors, and replacing text.

Use the Format Cells Dialog Box and Apply Borders and Fills to Cells

1. Start **Excel**. Open **EX05-A02-CustomerBase** from the **EX2013 Lesson 05** folder and save it as **EX05-A02-CustomerBase-[FirstInitialLastName]**.

2. Use the Format Cells dialog box to format **cell E19** with **Bold** and **Italic** font style.

3. Place a **single border** along the bottom of the **range A2:F2** and a **double border** along the bottom of **cell E19**.

   A bottom double border is often used to denote the final figure on a worksheet.

4. Apply a Standard Orange fill color to the merged **range A1:F1**.

Use Excel's Find and Replace Commands

5. Find all instances of **projects** and replace with **Jobs**.

6. Find all instances of **project** and replace with **Job**.

7. Find all instances of **Currency** number formatting and replace with **Accounting** number formatting.

   This is an efficient way to make the same formatting change to multiple cells.

8. Save and then close the file; exit from **Excel**.

9. Submit your final file based on the guidelines provided by your instructor.

   To view examples of how your file or files should look at the end of this exercise, go to the student resource center.

APPLY YOUR SKILLS EX05-A03

Format an Event Listing

In this exercise, you will format both text and numbers within an event listing.

Format Worksheets and Use Excel's Alignment and Indent Features

1. Start **Excel**. Open **EX05-A03-EventListing** from the **EX2013 Lesson 05** folder and save it as **EX05-A03-EventListing-[FirstInitialLastName]**.

2. Apply **bold** formatting to the entries in **rows 5 and 15**.

3. Format the title in **cell A1** with **bold**, and change the font size to **14**.

4. Right-align the entries in the **range B5:D5**.

5. Indent the entry in **cell A15**.

Use Excel's Text Control Options and Format Numbers

6. Merge and center the title in **cell A1** across **columns A–D**.

7. **Merge Across** the titles in the **range A2:A3**; center the contents so they appear consistent with the title in row 1.

8. Insert a **line break** in **cell A11** so *Southwestern* is on a separate line.
   This line break was necessary, since the cell contents extended into column B.

9. Format the **range B6:D15** in **Currency Style** with **two decimals**.

10. Format **cell B17** in **Number** style with **zero decimals**.

Use the Format Cells Dialog Box and Apply Borders and Fills to Cells

11. Use the Format Cells dialog box to format **cell B17** with **Bold** and **Standard Red** font.

12. Place a **single border** along the bottom of the **range B5:D5** and a **top and double bottom border** on the **range B15:D15**.

13. Apply a Standard Yellow fill color to the merged cells in the **range A1:D3**.
    Fill color should be used sparingly in a worksheet, as too much color can give a scattered appearance.

Use Excel's Find and Replace Commands

14. Find all instances of **job** and replace with **Event**.

15. Find all instances of **Currency** number formatting and replace with **Accounting** number formatting.
    30 replacements are made here, as every cell in the range B6:D15, regardless of whether it contained data, previously had Currency formatting.

16. Save and then close the file; exit from **Excel**.

17. Submit your final file based on the guidelines provided by your instructor.

Extend Your Skills

In the course of working through the Extend Your Skills exercises, you will think critically as you use the skills taught in the lesson to complete the assigned projects. To evaluate your mastery and completion of the exercises, your instructor may use a rubric, with which more points are allotted according to performance characteristics. (The more you do, the more you earn!) Ask your instructor how your work will be evaluated.

EX05-E01 That's the Way I See It

You are making a list of the five charities to which you are most likely to donate a little extra cash in your pocket. The list will include the charity name, the cause that it supports, and the total donations that the charity received last year.

Create a new file in the **EX2013 Lesson 05** folder named **EX05-E01-Charity-[FirstInitialLastName]**.

Enter a header at the top of the worksheet and headers for each column that you create. Use text and number formats to improve the appearance of the worksheet, and place a fill color in the cell of the charity that you would be most likely to support. Conduct an Internet search to determine the information for each charity in order to complete the worksheet (you may enter a "best guess" estimate for any donation totals you are unable to locate).

You will be evaluated based on the inclusion of all elements specified, your ability to follow directions, your ability to apply newly learned skills to a real-world situation, your creativity, and the relevance of your topic and/or data choice(s). Submit your final file based on the guidelines provided by your instructor.

EX05-E02 Be Your Own Boss

You are working on the income statement for your company, Blue Jean Landscaping, for the month of July 2013.

Open **EX05-E02-IncomeStatement** from the **EX2013 Lesson 05** folder and save it as **EX05-E02-IncomeStatement-[FirstInitialLastName]**.

The file contains all necessary data to complete the income statement. Using the techniques you learned in this lesson, apply all borders, indents, and number formats required to properly format an income statement. If necessary, refer to the Develop Your Skills exercise within the main part of the lesson to identify the proper formatting. Use the Find and Replace dialog box to change all instances of *Costs* within the worksheet to *Expenses*.

You will be evaluated based on the inclusion of all elements specified, your ability to follow directions, your ability to apply newly learned skills to a real-world situation, your creativity, and your demonstration of an entrepreneurial spirit. Submit your final file based on the guidelines provided by your instructor.

Transfer Your Skills

In the course of working through the Transfer Your Skills exercises, you will use critical-thinking and creativity skills to complete the assigned projects using skills taught in the lesson. To evaluate your mastery and completion of the exercises, your instructor may use a rubric, with which more points are allotted according to performance characteristics. (The more you do, the more you earn!) Ask your instructor how your work will be evaluated.

EX05-T01 Use the Web as a Learning Tool

Throughout this book, you will be provided with an opportunity to use the Internet as a learning tool by completing WebQuests. According to the original creators of WebQuests, as described on their website (WebQuest.org), a WebQuest is "an inquiry-oriented activity in which most or all of the information used by learners is drawn from the web." To complete the WebQuest projects in this book, navigate to the student resource center and choose the WebQuest for the lesson on which you are currently working. The subject of each WebQuest will be relevant to the material found in the lesson.

WebQuest Subject: Create an ingredient spreadsheet to facilitate weekly orders

Submit your final file(s) based on the guidelines provided by your instructor.

EX05-T02 Demonstrate Proficiency

You have determined that to maximize revenue for Stormy BBQ you will need to fully examine local competing restaurants. Your evaluation will help you determine which local restaurants appeal to your customers and what dishes on their menus are most similar to yours.

Open **EX05-T02-Restaurants** from the **EX2013 Lesson 05** folder and save it as **EX05-T02-Restaurants-[FirstInitialLastName]**. Format your worksheet using techniques such as Merge & Center, Wrap Text, indentations, bold text, and borders. Also, determine which dishes are most like those at Stormy BBQ and apply green fill to the corresponding cells. Write a paragraph with at least five sentences in the cell below your data that explains what you see in the data—which restaurant is your biggest competitor, what dishes are the most similar to your own, and what action you might take based on this data. Merge and center the paragraph to extend across your entire data set.

Submit your final file based on the guidelines provided by your instructor.

EXCEL 2013

Charting Worksheet Data

Charting is an important skill to have when using worksheets because comparisons, trends, and other relationships are often conveyed more effectively with charts than by displaying only data. In this lesson, you will use Excel to create column charts, line charts, and pie charts. You will edit and format legends, data labels, and other chart objects. You will also add trendlines and sparklines to worksheets.

LESSON OUTLINE

LEARNING OBJECTIVES

After studying this lesson, you will be able to:

- Create different types of charts
- Move and size embedded charts
- Modify and format chart elements
- Create trendlines and sparklines
- Preview and print worksheets

Charting Sales Performance

You have been asked to prepare several charts for Green Clean, which sells janitorial products and contracts for cleaning services. You will prepare charts that compare sales in the various quarters, display the growth trend throughout the year, and illustrate the contributions of each sales team member to the company sales as a whole. You will use Excel's charting features to produce accurate and easy-to-understand visuals that meet Green Clean's high standards.

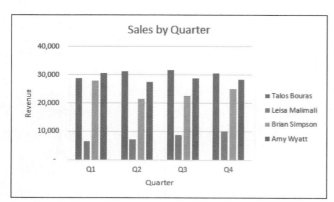

A column chart

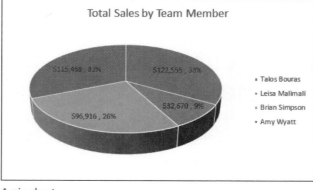

A pie chart

A line chart

Creating Charts in Excel

Video Library http://labyrinthelab.com/videos   Video Number: EX13-V0601

Many people are "visual learners" and find that numerical data is easier to interpret when presented in a chart. Charts are linked to the data from which they are created, thus charts are automatically updated when worksheet data changes. You can apply options and enhancements to each chart element, such as the title, legend, plot area, value axis, category axis, and data series.

Chart Placement

You have the option of either embedding a new chart into the worksheet where the data resides or placing it on a separate sheet. This can be done when the chart is first created, or at any time thereafter.

Embedded charts can be created by choosing the chart type from the Insert tab. To avoid covering the worksheet data, you can move and resize an embedded chart.

FROM THE KEYBOARD
F11 to create a chart on its own sheet

You can use the F11 key to place a full-size chart on its own sheet. When you do, the chart on the new sheet will be based on the default chart type. You can easily change the type after creating the chart with the Change Chart Type option.

Choosing the Proper Data Source

It is important to select both the appropriate data, and the proper row and column headings for your column and bar charts to make sure the data are accurate. Usually, you will not include both individual category data and totals because the individual data would appear distorted.

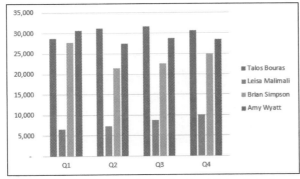
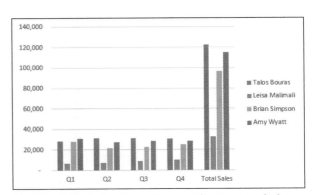

The column chart that excludes the Total Sales data does a better job of displaying the differences between each data series.

Chart Types

Excel provides 10 major chart types, as well as several subtypes for each. Each chart type represents data in a different manner, and you can also create a customized chart (which can be used as a template) to meet your exact needs.

FROM THE RIBBON

Insert→Charts→
Recommended Charts

Chart and Axis Titles

Excel allows you to create titles for your charts as well as for the value and category axes. If you choose a range of information that includes what appears to Excel to be a title, Excel will include it in the new chart.

	Column
	Line
	Pie
	Bar
	Area
	X Y (Scatter)
	Stock
	Surface
	Radar
	Combo

◢	A	B	C	D	E	F
2	Quarterly and Total Sales - Fiscal Year					
3						
4		Q1	Q2	Q3	Q4	Total Sales
5	Talos Bouras	28,775	31,342	31,763	30,675	$ 122,555
6	Leisa Malimali	6,575	7,304	8,768	10,023	$ 32,670
7	Brian Simpson	27,850	21,471	22,634	24,961	$ 96,916
8	Amy Wyatt	30,725	27,444	28,802	28,497	$ 115,468
10	Quarter Total	$ 93,925	$ 87,561	$ 91,967	$ 94,156	$ 367,609

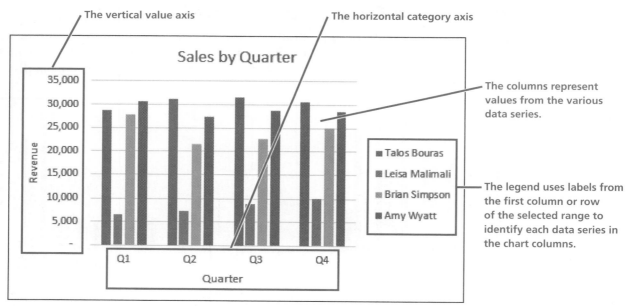

This column chart compares values using vertical bars. It was created using the highlighted worksheet data.

Chart Formatting Control

To quickly preview and select different chart elements, styles, and filters, you can use the chart formatting buttons that appear when a chart is selected. When you scroll over an option within any of the three buttons, its appearance will be previewed within your chart.

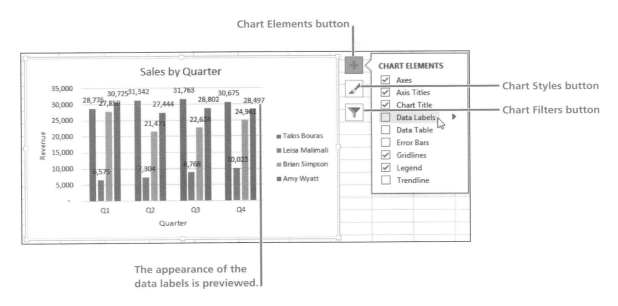

Chart Elements button

The appearance of the data labels is previewed.

Chart Styles button

Chart Filters button

QUICK REFERENCE	CREATING AND PLACING A CHART
Task	**Procedure**
Create a chart	▪ Select the desired data range and choose the chart type from Insert→Charts.
Move an existing chart to its own sheet	▪ Right-click a blank area of the chart and choose Move Chart. ▪ Choose New Sheet, rename the sheet, and click OK.
Move a chart from its own sheet to another sheet as an embedded object	▪ Right-click a blank area of the chart and choose Move Chart. ▪ Choose Object In, select the desired worksheet, and click OK.
Add a title to a chart	▪ Select the desired chart. ▪ Choose Chart Tools→Design→Chart Layouts→Add Chart Element 📊→Chart Title and select a chart title option. ▪ Select the default title "Chart Title" and type in your title.
Add axis titles to a chart	▪ Select the desired chart. ▪ Choose Chart Tools→Design→Chart Layouts→Add Chart Element 📊→Axis Titles and select an axis title option. ▪ Select the default title "Axis Title" and type your title.
Add a legend to a chart	▪ Select the desired chart. ▪ Choose Chart Tools→Design→Chart Layouts→Add Chart Element 📊→Legend and select a legend option.

Create a Chart

In this exercise, you will create an embedded clustered bar chart.

1. Open **EX06-D01-SalesCharts** from the **EX2013 Lesson 06** folder and save it as **EX06-D01-SalesCharts-[FirstInitialLastName]**.

   Replace the bracketed text with your first initial and last name. For example, if your name is Bethany Smith, your filename would look like this: EX06-D01-SalesChart-BSmith.

2. Select the **range A4:E8** in the **Sales by Quarter** worksheet.

3. Tap the F11 key.

   Tapping F11 creates a new sheet before the Sales by Quarter sheet in the workbook tab order.

4. Double-click the new chart tab, type **Sales by Rep**, and tap Enter.

Create a Clustered Bar Chart

5. Display the **Sales by Quarter** worksheet and make certain the **range A4:E8** is still selected.

6. Follow these steps to create a clustered bar chart:

   Ⓐ Click the **Insert** tab.

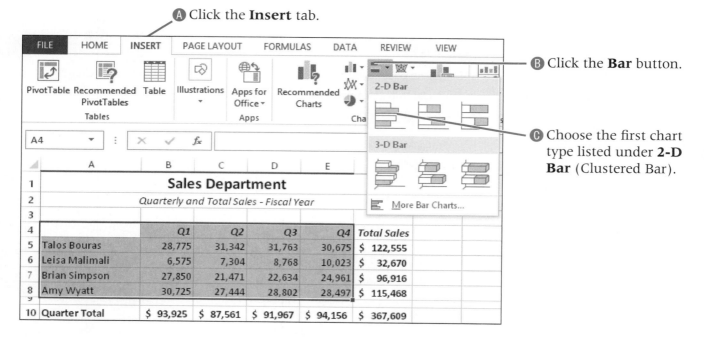

   Ⓑ Click the **Bar** button.

   Ⓒ Choose the first chart type listed under **2-D Bar** (Clustered Bar).

   The chart will appear embedded in the Sales by Quarter worksheet with the default properties for the clustered bar chart type displayed.

7. Look at the Ribbon to see that the **Chart Tools** are now displayed and the **Design** tab is active.

   The additional Ribbon tabs under Chart Tools, which appear when a chart is selected, are referred to as contextual tabs.

Edit the Chart and Axis Titles

8. Follow these steps to title the chart:

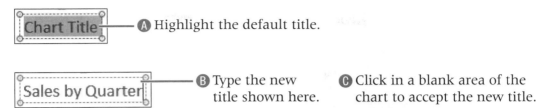

Ⓐ Highlight the default title.

Ⓑ Type the new title shown here.

Ⓒ Click in a blank area of the chart to accept the new title.

Instead of highlighting the title, you could have clicked the default title. However, the new title would have only displayed on the formula bar as you typed.

9. Remaining within the chart, follow these steps to add a vertical axis title:

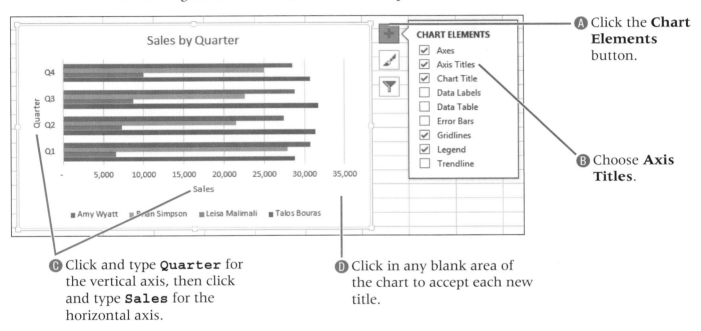

Ⓐ Click the **Chart Elements** button.

Ⓑ Choose **Axis Titles**.

Ⓒ Click and type **Quarter** for the vertical axis, then click and type **Sales** for the horizontal axis.

Ⓓ Click in any blank area of the chart to accept each new title.

10. Save the file and leave it open; you will modify it throughout this lesson.

Moving and Sizing Embedded Charts

Video Library   http://labyrinthelab.com/videos   Video Number: EX13-V0602

When a chart is selected, it is surrounded by a light border with sizing handles displayed. A selected chart can be both moved and resized.

Moving Embedded Charts

Charts that are embedded in a worksheet can easily be moved to a new location. A chart can be moved by a simple drag, but you need to ensure that you click the chart area and not a separate element.

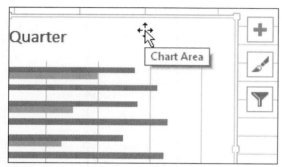

A four-pointed arrow (along with the "Chart Area" ScreenTip) indicates that you can drag to move this selected chart.

Sizing Embedded Charts

To size a chart, it must first be selected. You can drag a sizing handle when the double-arrow mouse pointer is displayed. To change a chart size proportionately, hold [Shift] while dragging a corner handle. If you wanted to only change the height or width of a chart you would not hold [Shift].

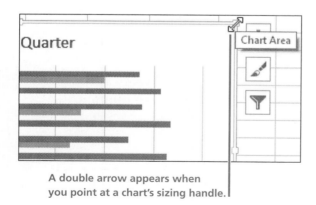

A double arrow appears when you point at a chart's sizing handle.

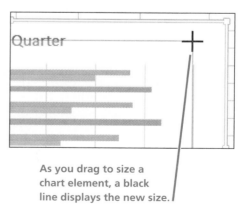

As you drag to size a chart element, a black line displays the new size.

Deleting Charts

Deleting an embedded chart is simple—just select the chart area and tap ⌊Delete⌋. You can delete a chart that is on its own tab by deleting the worksheet.

Size and Move an Embedded Chart

In this exercise, you will move and resize your chart. You will also copy a sheet containing an embedded chart and then delete the chart.

1. Save your file as **EX06-D02-SalesCharts-[FirstInitialLastName]**.

2. Click once on the chart area of the embedded chart in the **Sales by Quarter** sheet to select the chart.
   Sizing handles appear around the border of the chart.

3. Follow these steps to resize the chart to be smaller:

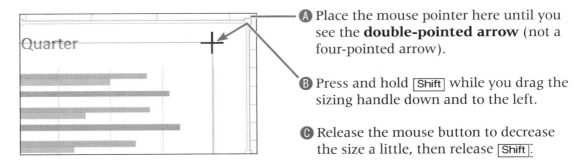

Ⓐ Place the mouse pointer here until you see the **double-pointed arrow** (not a four-pointed arrow).

Ⓑ Press and hold ⌊Shift⌋ while you drag the sizing handle down and to the left.

Ⓒ Release the mouse button to decrease the size a little, then release ⌊Shift⌋.

Excel resized the width and height proportionately because you held down the ⌊Shift⌋ key as you resized the chart.

4. Follow these steps to move the chart and center it below the worksheet data:

Ⓐ Place the mouse pointer over a blank area of the chart so that a **four-pointed arrow** appears.

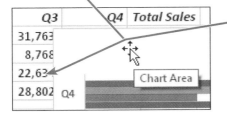

Ⓑ Drag the chart down and to the left until it is just below **row 11** and centered within **columns A–F.**

Ⓒ Release the mouse button.

Excel 2013

5. Hold down [Ctrl], drag the **Sales by Quarter** sheet tab to the right, and then release the mouse and [Ctrl].

The downward-pointing arrow that indicates the location of the new sheet may not appear if the chart is positioned over it. The duplicate sheet is named Sales by Quarter (2).

6. Rename the **Sales by Quarter (2)** sheet to `Team Totals`.

Delete an Embedded Chart

7. Click once to select the chart in the **Team Totals** sheet and tap [Delete].
   Excel deletes the chart.

8. Use [Ctrl]+[Z] to undo the Delete command.
   The chart reappears. You can restore an embedded chart right after it is deleted.

9. Use [Ctrl]+[Y] to redo the Delete command.
   The chart is once again deleted.

10. Save the file and leave it open.

Exploring Other Chart Types

Video Library   http://labyrinthelab.com/videos   Video Number: EX13-V0603

Here you will explore line and pie charts and how they can make your data work for you. Pie charts are suitable when you are examining data that represent portions of a whole (just as pieces of an apple pie, when combined, represent the whole pie).

Line Charts

Line charts are most useful for comparing trends over a period of time. Like column charts, line charts have category and value axes. Line charts also use the same or similar objects as column charts.

	A	B	C	D	E	F
1	**Sales Department**					
2	*Quarterly and Total Sales - Fiscal Year*					
3						
4		*Q1*	*Q2*	*Q3*	*Q4*	*Total Sales*
5	Talos Bouras	28,775	31,342	31,763	30,675	$ 122,555
6	Leisa Malimali	6,575	7,304	8,768	10,023	$ 32,670
7	Brian Simpson	27,850	21,471	22,634	24,961	$ 96,916
8	Amy Wyatt	30,725	27,444	28,802	28,497	$ 115,468
10	Quarter Total	$ 93,925	$ 87,561	$ 91,967	$ 94,156	$ 367,609

The chart was created using the selected data.

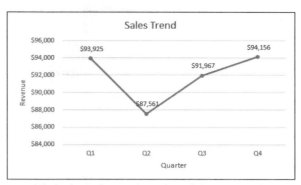

Data labels show the precise value of the various data points.

Pie Charts

You typically select only two sets of data when creating pie charts: the values to be represented by the pie slices and the labels to identify the slices.

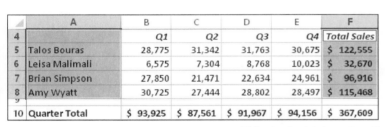

	A	B	C	D	E	F
4		*Q1*	*Q2*	*Q3*	*Q4*	*Total Sales*
5	Talos Bouras	28,775	31,342	31,763	30,675	$ 122,555
6	Leisa Malimali	6,575	7,304	8,768	10,023	$ 32,670
7	Brian Simpson	27,850	21,471	22,634	24,961	$ 96,916
8	Amy Wyatt	30,725	27,444	28,802	28,497	$ 115,468
10	Quarter Total	$ 93,925	$ 87,561	$ 91,967	$ 94,156	$ 367,609

This pie chart is based on the selected data.

Exploding Pie Slices

There will be times when you want to draw attention to a particular slice of a pie chart. You can make one slice explode from the chart simply by dragging it away from the other slices.

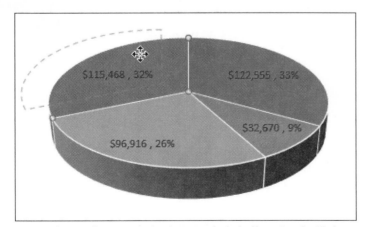

As you drag a slice out to give it an exploded effect, Excel will show with a dashed line where it will land.

Rotating and Elevating Pie Charts

You can change the rotation and perspective (also known as elevation) of pie charts to display data in a different position or change the angle at which it is viewed.

FROM THE RIBBON

Format→Shape
Styles→Shape
Effects→3-D
Rotation→3-D Rotation
Options

You can rotate other types of 3-D charts as well, but 2-D charts cannot be rotated.

DEVELOP YOUR SKILLS EX06-D03
Create a Line Chart

In this exercise, you will use the same data to create a line chart and a pie chart.

1. Save your file as **EX06-D03-SalesCharts-[FirstInitialLastName]**.

2. Select the **Sales by Quarter** worksheet.

3. Follow these steps to select the data for the line chart:

Ⓐ Select the **range A4:E4**.

Ⓑ Press and hold [Ctrl] while selecting the **range A10:E10**.

Ⓒ Choose **Insert→Charts→Insert Line Chart ▼ →Line with Markers**.

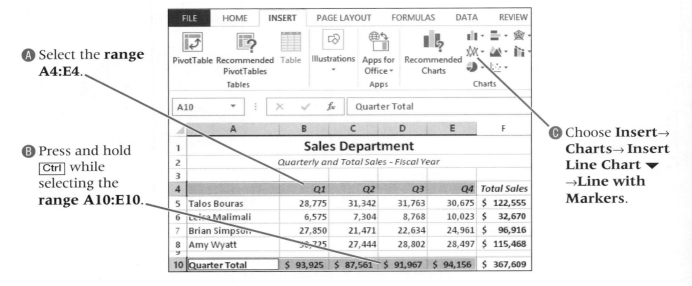

Excel creates an embedded line chart in the current worksheet.

4. With the chart selected, choose **Chart Tools→Design→Location→Move Chart** 🔲.

5. Follow these steps to move the chart to its own sheet:

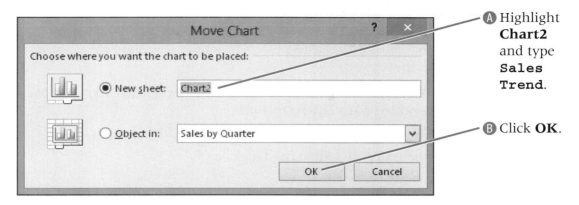

Ⓐ Highlight **Chart2** and type **Sales Trend**.

Ⓑ Click **OK**.

The chart now appears on its own worksheet.

Edit the Chart

6. Click the **Title** text box, type **Sales Trend**, and tap Enter.

7. Choose **Chart Tools→Design→Chart Layouts→Add Chart Element** ⯈**→Axis Titles→Primary Horizontal**.

   A text box appears below the horizontal axis with the default name Axis Title.

8. Type **Quarter** and tap Enter to replace the default horizontal axis title.

9. Choose **Chart Tools→Design→Chart Layouts→Add Chart Element** ⯈**→Axis Titles→Primary Vertical**, type **Revenue**, and tap Enter.

10. Choose **Chart Tools→Design→Chart Layouts→Add Chart Element** ⯈**→Data Labels→Above**.

   Excel displays the values above the data points on the chart.

Insert a Pie Chart

11. Select the **Team Totals** worksheet.

12. Follow these steps to select the range for the pie chart:

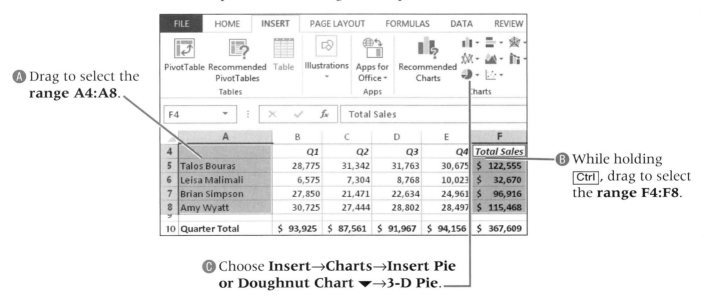

Ⓐ Drag to select the **range A4:A8**.

Ⓑ While holding Ctrl, drag to select the **range F4:F8**.

Ⓒ Choose **Insert→Charts→Insert Pie or Doughnut Chart** ▼**→3-D Pie**.

13. Place the mouse pointer over the chart area so that the **four-pointed arrow** appears, and then drag down and left until it is below **row 11** and centered between **columns A–F**.

    Notice that the cell F4 entry, Total Sales, *is used as the chart title.*

14. Edit the chart title to read **Total Sales by Team Member**. Click outside of the Title box to accept the new title.

15. Choose **Chart Tools→Design→Chart Layouts→Add Chart Element** ▮▮ **→Data Labels→More Data Label Options**.

    The Format Data Labels task pane appears.

16. Follow these steps to format the data labels:

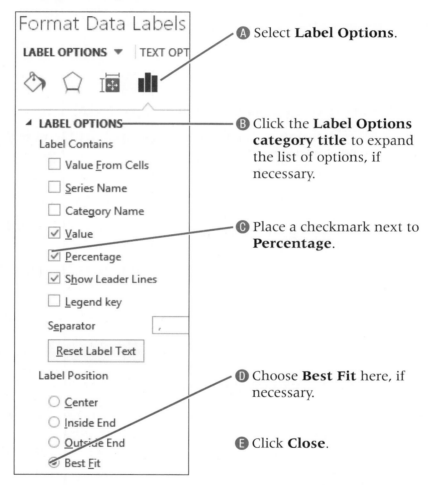

Ⓐ Select **Label Options**.

Ⓑ Click the **Label Options category title** to expand the list of options, if necessary.

Ⓒ Place a checkmark next to **Percentage**.

Ⓓ Choose **Best Fit** here, if necessary.

Ⓔ Click **Close**.

Excel displays both the value and the percentage in each pie slice wherever they "best fit."

Explode a Pie Slice

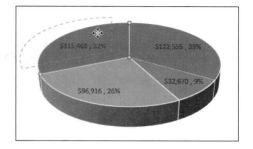

17. Click the slice representing **Amy Wyatt's sales**, and then pause and click it again.

    The first click will select all slices, and the second click will select just the slice for Amy Wyatt.

18. Place the mouse pointer over the **Amy Wyatt** slice until you see a move pointer, and then drag away from the pie chart slightly and release.

    Notice that as you drag the pie slice away from the main chart, a dashed line appears where the slice will land if you release the mouse button.

19. Save the file and leave it open.

Modifying Existing Charts

Video Library   http://labyrinthelab.com/videos   Video Number: EX13-V0604

You can modify any chart object after the chart has been created. The following table describes the various Chart Tools available to modify your charts.

CHART TOOLS ON THE RIBBON	
Contextual Tab	**Command Groups on the Tab**
Design	■ *Chart Layouts:* Change the overall layout of the chart and add chart elements.
	■ *Chart Styles:* Choose a preset style for your chart.
	■ *Data:* Switch the data displayed on rows and columns, and reselect the data for the chart.
	■ *Type:* Change the type of chart, set the default chart type, and save a chart as a template.
	■ *Location:* Switch a chart from being embedded to being placed on its own sheet and vice versa.
Format	■ *Current Selection:* Select a specific chart element, apply formatting, and reset formatting.
	■ *Insert Shapes:* Insert and change shapes.
	■ *Shape Styles:* Visually make changes to the selected chart element.
	■ *WordArt Styles:* Apply WordArt to text labels in your chart.
	■ *Arrange:* Change how your chart is arranged in relation to other objects in your worksheet.
	■ *Size:* Change the size of your chart.

Changing the Chart Type and Source Data

It's easy to change an existing chart to a different type using the Change Chart Type dialog box. You can also change the source data from within the Select Data Source dialog box. You may find it easier to edit the existing data range by using the collapse button. Aside from editing the data range, you can also alter individual data series, add additional data series, and alter the horizontal axis. Note that the Switch Row/Column option swaps the data in the vertical and horizontal axes.

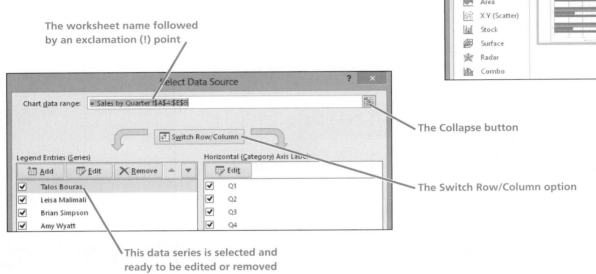

The worksheet name followed by an exclamation (!) point

The Collapse button

The Switch Row/Column option

This data series is selected and ready to be edited or removed

Using the arrow keys to edit a data range in a text box will result in unwanted characters. For best results, reselect a data range by dragging in the worksheet.

Modifying and Formatting Chart Elements

The legend, titles, and columns are chart elements. Once selected, you can delete, move, size, and format different elements. You can move a selected element by dragging it with the mouse when you see the move pointer, or change its size by dragging a sizing handle.

You can modify any chart element after the chart has been created by double-clicking the chart element to display a Format task pane with many options for that element. For example, options in the Format Chart Title dialog box allow you to adjust the vertical alignment, adjust the text direction, and apply a fill, border, or other visual effects.

Previewing Formatting Before Applying

The Chart Formatting buttons allow you to preview a variety of formatting changes. If you place the mouse pointer over an option accessed through these buttons, a preview displays how the change will look in your chart.

QUICK REFERENCE	MODIFYING EXISTING CHARTS
Task	**Procedure**
Change the chart type	▪ Select the chart, choose Chart Tools→Design→Type→Change Chart Type, and double-click the desired type.
Select a new data range for an entire chart	▪ Select the chart and choose Chart Tools→Design→Data→Select Data. ▪ Click the Collapse ⊞ button and select the new data range. ▪ Click the Expand ⊞ button and click OK.
Select a new range for a data series	▪ Select the chart and choose Chart Tools→Design→Data→Select Data. ▪ Select the desired item under the Legend Entries (Series) and click Edit. ▪ Highlight the Series Values entry, select the new range, and click OK twice.
Add additional data series	▪ Select the chart and choose Chart Tools→Design→Data→Select Data. ▪ Click Add under Legend Entries, enter the desired cell(s) for Series Name and Series Values, and click OK twice.
Delete a chart element	▪ Select the desired chart element and tap Delete.
Format an element on an existing chart	▪ Select the chart element and choose the desired formatting command.

DEVELOP YOUR SKILLS EX06-D04

Modify a Chart

In this exercise, you will change a chart type and then apply various formatting features to the new chart.

1. Save the file as **EX06-D04-SalesCharts-[FirstInitialLastName]**.

2. Select the **Sales by Rep** worksheet, click anywhere within the column chart, and choose **Chart Tools→Design→Type→Change Chart Type**.

   The Change Chart Type dialog box appears.

3. Follow these steps to change the chart type:

Ⓐ Display the **Bar** category.

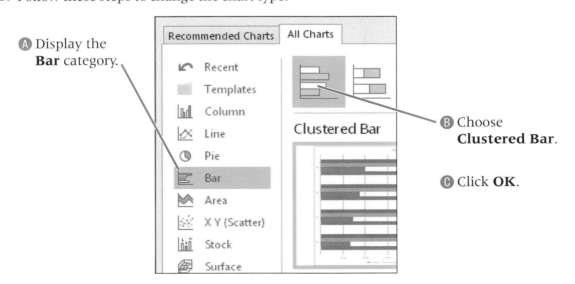

Ⓑ Choose **Clustered Bar**.

Ⓒ Click **OK**.

4. Choose **Chart Tools→Design→Data→Select Data** 🔲.

   You will now exclude the sales performance of Talos Bouras from the data range.

5. Follow these steps to reselect the chart data range:

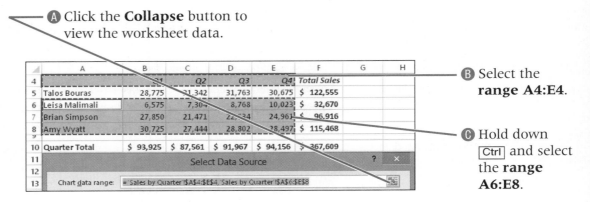

(A) Click the **Collapse** button to view the worksheet data.

(B) Select the **range A4:E4**.

(C) Hold down ⎡Ctrl⎤ and select the **range A6:E8**.

(D) Click the **Expand** 🔲 button and click **OK**.

   The Legend Entries (Series) now list Amy Wyatt, Brian Simpson, and Leisa Malimali.

6. Select one of the column bars for **Leisa Malimali** and tap ⎡Delete⎤.

   Now two data series display in the chart.

Format a Chart Using the Ribbon

7. Click anywhere within the top bar in the chart.

8. Follow these steps to apply formatting to the Amy Wyatt data series:

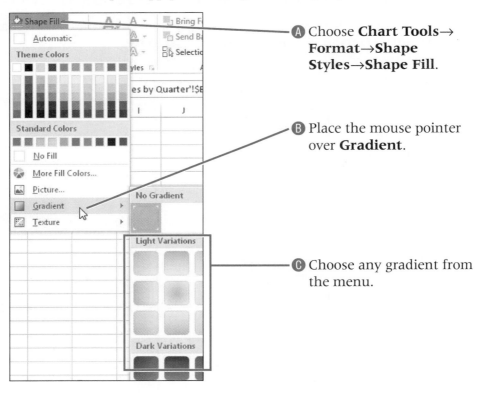

(A) Choose **Chart Tools→ Format→Shape Styles→Shape Fill**.

(B) Place the mouse pointer over **Gradient**.

(C) Choose any gradient from the menu.

9. Click anywhere within the chart area to select it.

Remember that any formatting you choose will apply only to the chart element selected.

10. Choose **Chart Tools→Format→Shape Styles→Shape Outline** ✐→**Weight** and select **3 pt**.

11. Choose **Chart Tools→Format→Shape Styles→Shape Outline** ✐ and apply any color; then, click away from the chart to review your formatting changes.

Format Axis Numbers

12. Double-click any of the values in the **horizontal axis**.

Be certain that the Format Axis task pane displays.

13. Follow these steps to format the axis numbers as Currency:

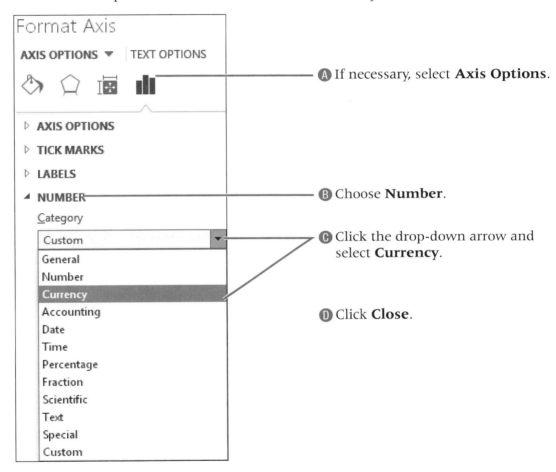

Ⓐ If necessary, select **Axis Options**.

Ⓑ Choose **Number**.

Ⓒ Click the drop-down arrow and select **Currency**.

Ⓓ Click **Close**.

14. Change the default chart title to `Sales by Rep`.

15. Save the file and leave it open.

Applying Layouts and Styles to Charts

Video Library http://labyrinthelab.com/videos Video Number: EX13-V0605

Chart layouts, also known as quick layouts, are designs that contain various preset chart elements. Choosing a chart layout saves time versus adding and formatting chart elements one at a time. Chart styles are based on the theme applied to your workbook. You can apply many preset styles to each chart type.

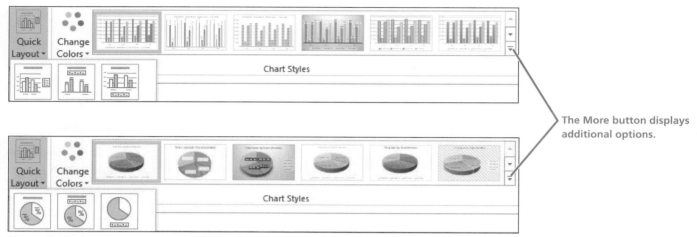

The More button displays additional options.

The available chart layouts and styles change based on the type of chart selected.

Formatting Attributes Controlled by the Selected Style

When you choose a style for your chart, the colors and effects (such as fill effects) change to match the style selected. Data in worksheet cells are not affected by any styles you apply to charts. Excel does not allow you to create your own styles, but you can save the formatting from a selected chart as a template to use as the basis for future charts.

QUICK REFERENCE	APPLYING A LAYOUT AND STYLE TO A CHART
Task	**Procedure**
Apply a layout or style to a chart	▪ Select the chart and click the Design tab.
	▪ Click Quick Layouts in the Chart Layouts group, or the More ⊽ button in the Chart Styles group, to display the available choices and make your selection.

Apply a Layout and a Style to a Chart

In this exercise, you will apply a quick layout and Chart Style to your bar chart.

1. Save your file as **EX06-D05-SalesCharts-[FirstInitialLastName]**.

2. Select the **Sales by Rep** sheet and choose **Page Layout→Themes→Themes** 🅰
 →**Organic**.

   A uniform color scheme, font set, and graphic effect are applied to the chart. If the worksheet contained additional data, it would have taken the new styles as well.

Change the Chart Layout

3. Click in the chart area of the **Sales by Rep** chart to select the chart, if necessary.

4. Choose **Chart Tools→Design→Chart Layouts→Quick Layout** 🖼.

   Excel displays all of the chart layout choices for this type of chart.

5. Choose **Layout 2** in the list.

   A ScreenTip displays the layout name as you point at each layout. When selecting a chart layout, you may need to reenter any title that is not within the data range specified for the chart.

Change the Chart Style

6. Choose **Chart Tools→Design→Chart Styles→ More** ⏷.

7. Choose **Style 4** in the list.

8. Save the file and leave it open.

Creating Trendlines

Video Library   http://labyrinthelab.com/videos   Video Number: EX13-V0606

Trendlines are used on charts for data analysis and prediction. A trendline displays the trend (increasing or decreasing) of one data series in a chart. There are several types of trendlines available, each suited to the display of particular data types. For example, a linear trendline works well with data that follow a fairly straight path. A moving average trendline will smooth out fluctuations in data by averaging two or more adjacent data points for each trendline data point.

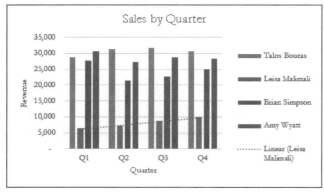

This linear trendline depicts the upward trend for Leisa Malimali's sales.

You cannot add a trendline to stacked, 3-D, or pie charts.

QUICK REFERENCE	CREATING TRENDLINES
Task	**Procedure**
Add a trendline to a chart	▪ Display the chart and choose Chart Tools→Design→Chart Layouts→Add Chart Element ▮▮→Trendline.
	▪ Choose a trendline type and select a data series to base it on (if necessary).
Change the trendline type	▪ Select the trendline.
	▪ Choose Chart Tools→Design→Chart Layouts→Add Chart Element ▮▮ →Trendline and select a trendline type.
Format the trendline	▪ Double-click the trendline and choose the desired option.

Add a Trendline

In this exercise, you will add a trendline to an existing chart.

1. Save your file as **EX06-D06-SalesCharts-[FirstInitialLastName]**.

2. Follow these steps to add a trendline to the Amy Wyatt data series:

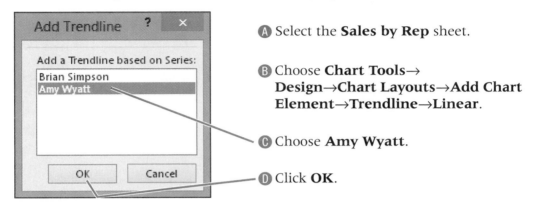

Ⓐ Select the **Sales by Rep** sheet.

Ⓑ Choose **Chart Tools→ Design→Chart Layouts→Add Chart Element→Trendline→Linear**.

Ⓒ Choose **Amy Wyatt**.

Ⓓ Click **OK**.

The trendline that appears shows the trend for Amy Wyatt only.

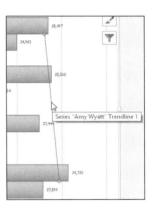

3. Position the tip of the pointer arrow against the trendline and click to select the trendline.

   Handles will display at the endpoints of the trendline.

4. Choose **Chart Tools→Design→Chart Layouts→Add Chart Element** 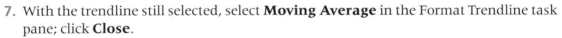**→Trendline→Linear Forecast**.

   The trendline lengthens to forecast sales in the next two quarters.

5. If necessary, double-click the trendline to open the **Format Trendline** task pane.

6. In the **Forecast** area of Trendline Options, change **Forward** from 2.0 periods to **1**; tap Enter.

   The trendline now forecasts only one quarter in the future.

7. With the trendline still selected, select **Moving Average** in the Format Trendline task pane; click **Close**.

   The trendline shortens to begin at the second quarter, omits the previously displayed forecast, and now displays an angle.

8. Save the file and leave it open.

Creating Sparklines in Cells

Video Library   http://labyrinthelab.com/videos   Video Number: EX13-V0607

Sparklines appear as miniature charts in worksheet cells. They allow you to show data graphically without creating a larger chart. You may select a cell range and create sparklines for every row or column at once. Changes to data are reflected immediately in sparklines adjacent to the data. Each sparkline charts the data in one row or column.

	A	B	C	D	E	F	G
4		*Q1*	*Q2*	*Q3*	*Q4*	*Total Sales*	
5	Talos Bouras	28,775	31,342	31,763	30,675	$ 122,555	
6	Leisa Malimali	6,575	7,304	8,768	10,023	$ 32,670	
7	Brian Simpson	27,850	21,471	22,634	24,961	$ 96,916	
8	Amy Wyatt	30,725	27,444	28,802	28,497	$ 115,468	

Sparklines show trends in data within a single cell.

Formatting Sparklines

You may format a sparkline as a line, column, or win-loss. The win-loss format shows whether figures are positive or negative. You may format sparklines with different styles and choose to display data points in various ways. Note that the same formatting must be applied to sparklines that were created all at once.

QUICK REFERENCE	CREATING SPARKLINES
Task	**Procedure**
Create a sparkline	■ Select the cell or cell range that will display the sparkline.
	■ Choose Insert→Sparklines and select the desired sparkline.
	■ Select the data range containing the source values and click OK.
Format a sparkline	■ Select the cell or range of cells containing the sparkline(s) and choose the desired option.

DEVELOP YOUR SKILLS EX06-D07
Create Sparklines

In this exercise, you will create sparklines to show upward and downward trends in data.

1. Save your file as **EX06-D07-SalesCharts-[FirstInitialLastName]**.

2. Display the **Team Totals** sheet and select the **range G5:G8**.
   These cells will contain the sparklines.

3. Choose **Insert→Sparklines →Line** 🗺.

4. Follow these steps to create the sparkline:

Ⓐ Move the dialog box, if necessary, to view **column B** in the worksheet.

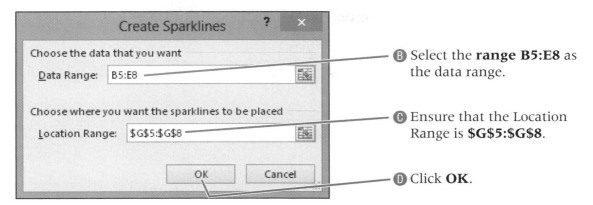

Ⓑ Select the **range B5:E8** as the data range.

Ⓒ Ensure that the Location Range is **$G$5:$G$8**.

Ⓓ Click **OK**.

Excel 2013

5. Choose **Sparkline Tools→Design→Show→Markers** to place a checkmark next to **Markers**.

The sparklines display a dot marker for each quarter, thus making the upward and downward trends easier to understand.

6. Select **cell G10** and then choose **Insert→Sparklines→Column** 📊.

7. In the **Create Sparklines** dialog box, set the Data Range to **B10:E10**, verify that the Location Range is **$G$10**, and click **OK**.

This time you created a single sparkline.

Format Sparklines

8. If necessary, select **cell G10**.

9. follow these steps to change the sparkline style:

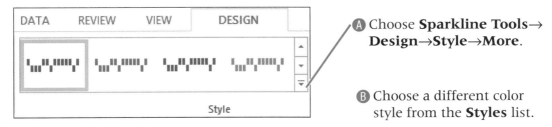

Ⓐ Choose **Sparkline Tools→ Design→Style→More**.

Ⓑ Choose a different color style from the **Styles** list.

10. Select **cell G5**.

The range G5:G8 is surrounded by an outline to indicate that the four sparklines are selected. You previously created these sparklines all at once.

11. Choose **Sparkline Tools→Design→Style→More** ⊟ button and choose a different style.

12. Save the file and leave it open.

Previewing and Printing Charts

Video Library   http://labyrinthelab.com/videos   Video Number: EX13-V0608

The print area within the File tab of Backstage view shows chart previews. Keep in mind that if an embedded chart is active when you choose to print, only the chart itself will print. You must deselect an embedded chart to print its entire worksheet.

Color fills and borders may not provide good contrast in charts printed on grayscale printers. Consider using shades of gray or black-and-white pattern fills.

QUICK REFERENCE	PRINTING CHARTS
Task	**Procedure**
Preview a chart	▪ Select the embedded chart or display the chart sheet.
	▪ Choose File→Print to see the preview in Backstage view.
Print a chart	▪ Select the embedded chart or display the chart sheet.
	▪ Choose File→Print, select printing options, and click print.

DEVELOP YOUR SKILLS EX06-D08
Preview and Print a Chart

In this exercise, you will preview the pie chart and print the line chart.

1. Save the file as **EX06-D08-SalesCharts-[FirstInitialLastName]**.

2. Select the **Team Totals** worksheet; then click once to select the pie chart.

3. Choose **File→Print**.

   The pie chart appears in the preview of the Print tab in Backstage view.

4. Tap Esc to exit Backstage view without printing.

5. Click in a cell away from the pie chart to deselect the chart.

6. Choose **File→Print**.

   Notice that when the chart is not selected, Excel will print the worksheet along with the embedded chart.

7. Tap Esc to exit Backstage view without printing.

8. Display the **Sales Trend** worksheet and, if desired, choose **File→Print** to print the worksheet.

9. Save then close the file. Exit **Excel**.

Concepts Review

To check your knowledge of the key concepts introduced in this lesson, complete the Concepts Review quiz by choosing the appropriate access option below.

If you are...	Then access the quiz by...
Using the Labyrinth Video Library	Going to http://labyrinthelab.com/videos
Using eLab	Logging in, choosing Content, and navigating to the Concepts Review quiz for this lesson
Not using the Labyrinth Video Library or eLab	Going to the student resource center for this book

Reinforce Your Skills

Create and Modify a Column Chart

In this exercise, you will create, move, and modify a column chart that compares total new customers by time period.

Create Charts in Excel

1. Start **Excel**. Open **EX06-R01-Comparison** from the **EX2013 Lesson 06** folder and save it as **EX06-R01-Comparison-[FirstInitialLastName]**.

2. Select the **range A3:E7**.

3. Choose **Insert→Charts→Column→2-D Column→Stacked Column**.

   The chart shows a column for each quarter with the four customer source categories stacked in each.

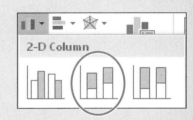

Move and Size Embedded Charts

4. Point at the chart area, and then drag the chart down and left until the upper-left corner is at **cell A11**.

5. Choose **Chart Tools→Design→Chart Layouts→Quick Layout→Layout 3**.

   ScreenTips help you locate Layout 3 in the list. The legend is moved below the horizontal axis and a title text box is added above the chart.

Explore Other Chart Types

6. Choose **Chart Tools→Design→Type→Change Chart Type→Line→Stacked Line**.

   After reviewing the stacked line chart, you decide that you prefer the stacked column chart.

7. Click **Undo** ↩.

Modify Existing Charts

8. Select the chart title text box, type **=**, select **cell A3**, and tap Enter.

   As you type the formula, =Contracts!$A$3 appears within the Formula Bar.

9. Choose **Chart Tools→Design→Data→Switch Row/Column**.

   The data reverse so the horizontal category axis displays the customer source categories. Each column represents the total new customers in a customer source category.

10. Save and then close the file. Exit **Excel**.

11. Submit your final file based on the guidelines provided by your instructor.

    To view examples of how your file or files should look at the end of this exercise, go to the student resource center.

Finalize and Preview a Chart

In this exercise, you will add a trendline to an existing chart and add sparklines to existing data. You will also apply a chart layout and preview a chart's appearance prior to printing.

Apply Layouts and Styles to Charts

1. Start **Excel**. Open **EX06-R02-PayrollExpenses** from the **EX2013 Lesson 06** folder and save it as **EX06-R02-PayrollExpenses-[FirstInitialLastName]**.

2. Select the chart then choose **Chart Tools→Design→Chart Styles→Style #9**.

3. Choose **Chart Tools→Design→Chart Layouts→Quick Layout→Layout #1**.

4. Change the default chart title text to **Payroll Expenses Chart** and click elsewhere on the worksheet to confirm the new title.

5. Using the ⎡Ctrl⎤ key, select the **range B3:E3** and the **range B9:E9**.

6. Choose **Insert→Charts→Insert Pie or Doughnut Chart→2-D Pie→Pie**.

7. Move the chart to **row 11** below the worksheet data.

8. Click the **Chart Elements** button for the pie chart and hold your mouse pointer over **Data Labels**. Click the arrow that appears and choose **More Options**.

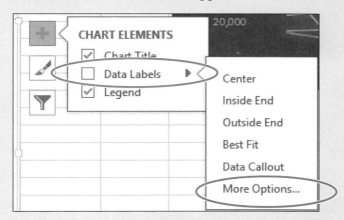

9. Under **Label Options**, place a checkmark next to **Category Name** and **Percentage**, remove the checkmark from **Value**, and click **Close**.

   If you had removed the checkmark from Value first, you would have immediately removed all data labels, which would have made the Label Options menu disappear.

10. Click the **Chart Elements** button for the pie chart, hold your mouse pointer over **Data Labels**, click the arrow, and choose **Inside End**.

11. Click in the legend for the pie chart and tap ⎡Delete⎤.

    The legend is unnecessary because the department names are displayed in the data labels.

12. Change the default chart title text for the pie chart to read **Payroll Expenses by Department**. Click elsewhere on the worksheet to confirm the new title.

Excel 2013

Create Trendlines

13. Select the **Payroll Expenses Chart** and choose **Chart Tools→Design→Chart Layouts→Add Chart Element→Trendline→More Trendline Options**.

14. Choose to apply the trendline to the **Wages** data series and then close the Format Trendline task pane.

Notice how the trendline has smoothed out the fluctuations in the Wages data series.

Create Sparklines in Cells

15. Select the **range G4:G8**.

16. Choose **Insert→Sparklines→Line** 〔⋊〕, select the **range B4:E8**, and click **OK**.

The Sparkline Tools Design tab appears when the sparklines are inserted.

17. Choose **Sparkline Tools→Design→Show** and click to place checkmarks beside **Markers** and **Low Point**.

The markers indicate each department.

18. Choose **Sparkline Tools→Design→Style→Marker Color→Low Point** and choose a different theme color.

Preview and Print Charts

19. With the pie chart selected, choose **File→Print**.

Only the chart is previewed in Backstage view because the pie chart is selected.

20. Tap 〔Esc〕 to exit Backstage view without printing.

21. Save and then close the file. Exit **Excel**.

22. Submit your final file based on the guidelines provided by your instructor.

To view examples of how your file or files should look at the end of this exercise, go to the student resource center.

REINFORCE YOUR SKILLS EX06-R03

Create and Finalize a Chart

In this exercise, you will create, move, and modify a bar chart. You will also add trendlines and sparklines, and preview the worksheet.

Create Charts in Excel

1. Start **Excel**. Open **EX06-R03-Donations** from the **EX2013 Lesson 06** folder and save it as **EX06-R03-Donations-[FirstInitialLastName]**.

2. Select the **range A3:E7**.

3. Choose **Insert→Charts→Insert Bar Chart→2-D Bar→Clustered Bar**.

The chart shows a cluster of four bars for each quarter. The bars represent the source of each donation.

Move and Size Embedded Charts

4. Point at the chart area and drag the chart down and to the left until the upper-left corner is at **cell A10**.

5. Hold ⎡Shift⎤, point at the bottom-right corner of the chart, and drag to reduce the chart size so it does not extend beyond **column F.**

Holding the ⎡Shift⎤ *key ensures that the chart will resize proportionally.*

Explore Other Chart Types

6. Choose **Chart Tools→Design→Type→Change Chart Type→Line→Line with Markers**; click **OK**.

After reviewing the line chart, you decide that you prefer the clustered bar chart.

7. Click **Undo** ⎡↩⎤.

Modify Existing Charts

8. Click in the chart title text box and type **Donation Source**. Click elsewhere in the worksheet to confirm the new title.

9. With the chart selected, choose **Chart Tools→Design→Chart Layouts→Add Chart Element→Legend→Top**.

10. Choose **Chart Tools→Design→Chart Layouts→Add Chart Element→Gridlines→ Primary Minor Vertical**.

Gridlines make it easier to determine the precise value of each bar within the chart.

Apply Layouts and Styles to Charts

11. Choose **Chart Tools→Design→Chart Styles→Style 2**.

12. Choose **Chart Tools→Design→Chart Layouts→Quick Layout** and review the available layouts.

If you had not already modified various chart elements, you could choose a layout here to alter multiple aspects at once.

Create Trendlines

13. Choose **Chart Tools→Design→Chart Layouts→Add Chart Element→Trendline→ Linear**.

14. Choose to apply the trendline to the **Web Orders** data series and click **OK**.

Create Sparklines in Cells

15. Select the **range G4:G7.**

16. Choose **Insert→Sparklines→Column** ⎡📊⎤, select the **range B4:E7** as the data range, and click **OK**.

The Sparkline Tools Design tab becomes accessible when the sparklines are inserted.

17. On the Design tab, change the style to **Sparkline Style Colorful #4**.

Preview and Print Charts

18. Choose **File→Print** to preview the worksheet.

19. Tap ⎡Esc⎤ to exit Backstage view without printing.

20. Save and then close the file. Exit **Excel**.

21. Submit your final file based on the guidelines provided by your instructor.

Apply Your Skills

Create a Line Chart

In this exercise, you will create a line chart on a separate sheet, rename the sheet tabs, and modify a chart.

Create Charts and Move and Size Embedded Charts in Excel

1. Start **Excel**. Start a new workbook and save it as **EX06-A01-WebOrders-[FirstInitialLastName]** in the **EX2013 Lesson 06** folder.

2. Create this worksheet using the following parameters:
   - Use **AutoFill** to expand the date series.
   - Resize the column widths as necessary.

3. Format the dates so they are displayed as Mar-14 (without the day).

4. Use the worksheet data to create the chart shown:
   - Set up the axis labels and title as shown.
   - Do not include a legend.

	A	B
1	Universal Corporate Events	
2	Web Orders	
3		
4	Date	Web Orders
5	3/15/2014	92
6	4/15/2014	146
7	5/15/2014	122
8	6/15/2014	154
9	7/15/2014	128
10	8/15/2014	140
11	9/15/2014	231
12	10/15/2014	245
13	11/15/2014	258
14	12/15/2014	244
15	1/15/2015	231
16	2/15/2015	176
17	Total	2,167

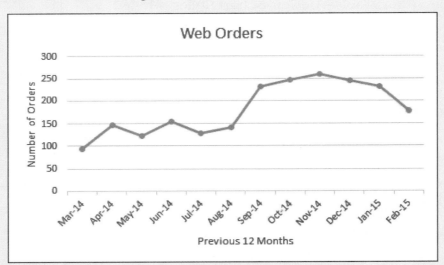

5. Place the chart on a separate sheet named **Web Orders Trend**.
   The dates will not appear slanted after the chart is moved.

6. Rename the **Sheet1** tab **Supporting Data**.

Explore Other Chart Types and Modify Existing Charts

7. Change chart type to a **3-D pie** chart.

   Since the data in this worksheet is not conveyed well in a pie chart, it's a good idea to change it once more.

8. Change chart type to a **3-D line** chart.

9. Remove the chart title and the **Depth (Series)** axis, which is displayed at the bottom-right of the chart.

10. Add a **legend** at the bottom of the chart.

    You can see that the legend lists only one data series, and therefore is not useful.

11. Click **Undo** to remove the legend.

12. Save and then close the file. Exit **Excel**.

13. Submit your final file based on the guidelines provided by your instructor.

    To view examples of how your file or files should look at the end of this exercise, go to the student resource center.

APPLY YOUR SKILLS EX06-A02

Present Data Using Multiple Methods

In this exercise, you will add sparklines, trendlines, and a column chart to a worksheet. You will also preview and print the worksheet.

Create Trendlines and Sparklines

1. Start **Excel**. Open **EX06-A02-ProjRev** from the **EX2013 Lesson 06** folder and save it as **EX06-A02-ProjRev-[FirstInitialLastName]**.

2. Use the data in the **range A6:F9** to create a **clustered column chart**.

3. Add a **linear trendline** to the **Revenue** data series.

4. Change the trendline to a **linear forecast trendline**.

5. Create **line sparklines** in **column G** to present the projected yearly changes in revenue, gross profit, and net profit.

6. Format the sparklines with **markers**.

Apply Layouts and Styles to Charts and Preview and Print Charts

7. Change the style of the chart to **Style 8**.

8. Change the layout of the chart to **Layout 10**.

   The layout change has deleted the trendline. Since you want to display the trendline, you need to undo the applied layout.

9. Click **Undo**.

10. Include the chart title **Financial Projections** and position the chart appropriately below the worksheet data.

11. Preview the worksheet and make any needed adjustments to the chart location.

12. Print the worksheet.

13. Save and then close the file. Exit **Excel**.

14. Submit your final file based on the guidelines provided by your instructor.

    To view examples of how your file or files should look at the end of this exercise, go to the student resource center.

Create a Column Chart and Edit Worksheets

In this exercise, you will create a column chart embedded in a worksheet. You will also move and print the chart and add sparklines to the worksheet.

Create Charts and Move and Size Embedded Charts in Excel

1. Start **Excel**. Start a new workbook and save it as **EX06-A03-NetIncome-[FirstInitialLastName]** in the **EX2013 Lesson 06** folder.

2. Create the worksheet and embedded column chart shown. Choose an appropriate chart layout so the negative numbers dip below the category axis in the chart.

The differences in row 6 are the revenues minus the expenses.

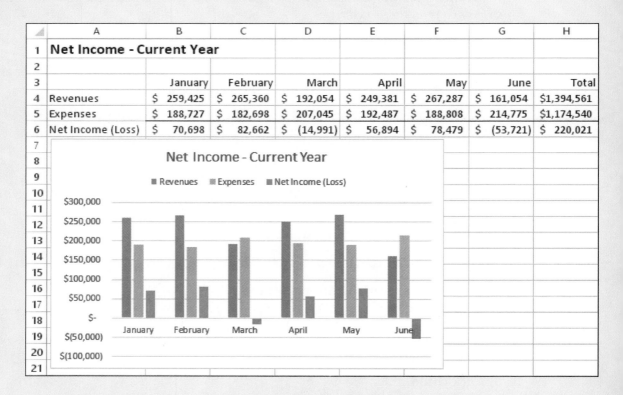

3. Move the chart to a separate sheet, and rename the sheet tab **Net Income Chart**.

4. Rename the worksheet tab **Net Income Analysis**.

5. Add the color of your choice to the **Net Income Analysis** tab.

Explore Other Chart Types and Modify Existing Charts

6. Create a **pie chart** on a separate sheet, showing revenues for the first six months of the year. Name the sheet **Revenue Chart**.

7. Explode the largest pie slice.

8. Change the chart colors of both charts to shades of gray, suitable for printing on a grayscale printer.

9. Italicize the chart titles of both charts.

Create Trendlines and Sparklines

10. Include a **linear trendline** within the column chart for **Net Income (Loss)**.

    Notice that the negative Net Income figures in March and June "drag" the trendline lower than it would be otherwise.

11. Within the Net Income Analysis tab, include **column sparklines** in column I for revenue, expenses, and net income.

12. Modify each sparkline to highlight the highest data point.

Apply Layouts and Styles to Charts and Preview and Print Charts

13. For the column chart, apply **Chart Style 5**.

14. For the pie chart, apply **Layout 6**.

15. Preview all three sheets within the workbook.

16. Print all three sheets in one step.

17. Save and close the file. Exit **Excel**.

18. Submit your final file based on the guidelines provided by your instructor.

Extend Your Skills

In the course of working through the Extend Your Skills exercises, you will think critically as you use the skills taught in the lesson to complete the assigned projects. To evaluate your mastery and completion of the exercises, your instructor may use a rubric, with which more points are allotted according to performance characteristics. (The more you do, the more you earn!) Ask your instructor how your work will be evaluated.

EX06-E01 That's the Way I See It

In this exercise, you will create a pie chart showing the box office receipts for the top five grossing movies from this past weekend. You can use the Internet to search for these figures, which should be readily available.

Create a new file named **EX06-E01-MovieGrosses-[FirstInitialLastName]** in the **EX2013 Lesson 06** folder.

Enter the box office data within your worksheet, making certain to include appropriate headers throughout. Create a pie chart based on the data and format the chart using the skills learned in this lesson. Explode the slice that represents your favorite movie of the weekend, apply an appropriate chart style, and move the chart to its own worksheet.

You will be evaluated based on the inclusion of all elements specified, your ability to follow directions, your ability to apply newly learned skills to a real-world situation, your creativity, and the relevance of your topic and/or data choice(s). Submit your final files based on the guidelines provided by your instructor.

EX06-E02 Be Your Own Boss

In this exercise, you will create and format sparklines for the equipment repair costs of your company, Blue Jean Landscaping.

Open **EX06-E02-RepairCost** from the **EX2013 Lesson 06** folder and save it as **EX06-E02-RepairCost-[FirstInitialLastName]**.

Use sparklines to show the cost trend for repairs on each of the three pieces of equipment. Apply a style and appropriate formatting to the sparklines. Then, type a paragraph (minimum of five sentences) in the row below your data to:

- Describe the purpose of the sparklines.
- Explain how sparklines can be used to evaluate your business's data.
- Detail what you have learned about Blue Jean Landscaping's equipment repair costs as a result of the sparklines.

Once you have completed the paragraph, print the data, including the sparklines and the paragraph, as a PDF, saving it as **EX06-E02-Sparklines-[FirstInitialLastName]**.

You will be evaluated based on the inclusion of all elements specified, your ability to follow directions, your ability to apply newly learned skills to a real-world situation, your creativity, and your demonstration of an entrepreneurial spirit. Submit your final files based on the guidelines provided by your instructor.

Transfer Your Skills

In the course of working through the Transfer Your Skills exercises, you will use critical-thinking and creativity skills to complete the assigned projects using skills taught in the lesson. To evaluate your mastery and completion of the exercises, your instructor may use a rubric, with which more points are allotted according to performance characteristics. (The more you do, the more you earn!) Ask your instructor how your work will be evaluated.

EX06-T01 Use the Web as a Learning Tool

Throughout this book, you will be provided with an opportunity to use the Internet as a learning tool by completing WebQuests. According to the original creators of WebQuests, as described on their website (WebQuest.org), a WebQuest is "an inquiry-oriented activity in which most or all of the information used by learners is drawn from the web." To complete the WebQuest projects in this book, navigate to the student resource center and choose the WebQuest for the lesson on which you are currently working. The subject of each WebQuest will be relevant to the material found in the lesson.

WebQuest Subject: Creating an appropriate chart based on worksheet data

Submit your final file(s) based on the guidelines provided by your instructor.

EX06-T02 Demonstrate Proficiency

Stormy BBQ's sales results are in! Your job is to chart the sales data so your manager can discuss the performance of each location in an upcoming team meeting.

Open **EX06-T02-SalesResults** from the **EX2013 Lesson 06** folder and save it as **EX06-T02-SalesResults-[FirstInitialLastName]**. Calculate the totals within the worksheet and consider the significant trends in sales performance. Create an embedded line chart with appropriate labeling for one of these trends. Show other worksheet results in a column chart on a separate sheet. Include a trendline within your column chart. Keep in mind the data relationships that each chart type can best display. When you have completed the charts, choose one of them and write a paragraph (minimum of 5 sentences) that summarizes the results for the team meeting. The summary should include how you plan to use the data to inform future decisions for the company and should be included on a separate worksheet.

Submit your final file based on the guidelines provided by your instructor.

Index

Notes

Notes

Notes

Notes

Notes

Notes